Sewing For Profits

By Judith & Allan Smith

NEW ADDRESS:

2812 BAYONNE DR.

PALM BEACH GARDENS, FL 33410

2nd Edition

ISBN-0-931113-01-6

Library of Congress Catalog Number: 84-051623

You may order single copies prepaid direct from the publisher for $10.00 + $1.00 for postage and handling.

SUCCESS ADVERTISING & PUBLISHING
8084 Nashua Drive, Lake Park, FL 33408

Illustration by Don Trachsler
Printing by Rose Publishing Company, Inc.,
      Tallahassee, Florida
Distribution by Success Advertising & Publishing

Printed in the United States of America

THIS BOOK IS WRITTEN FOR THOSE WHO WANT TO BE WINNERS!

FOR THOSE who have expanded beyond the normal 10% of their abilities

FOR THOSE who want to show the rest of the world they have talent

FOR THOSE who systematically want to organize themselves

FOR THOSE who want to grow, learn and adapt proven successful business basics

FOR THOSE who realize SUCCESS does not come easy

FOR THOSE ready to give that EXTRA EFFORT

FOR THOSE who want to have fun while making money

FOR THOSE who want to share their knowledge with others

FOR THOSE who realize that they will have to be a salesperson

FOR THOSE who won't quit with the first or second failure

WHAT KIND OF NUT IS SHE?

SHE WANTS TO RUN HER OWN BUSINESS
SHE WANTS TO SELECT HER OWN DOCTOR
SHE WANTS TO SELECT HER OWN FRIENDS
SHE WANTS TO BUY HER OWN INSURANCE
SHE WANTS TO SELECT HER OWN READING MATERIAL
SHE WANTS TO CREATE HER OWN SAVINGS PROGRAM
SHE WANTS TO SPEND HER OWN MONEY
SHE WANTS TO DO HER OWN THING
SHE WANTS TO EDUCATE HER CHILDREN THE WAY SHE SEES FIT
SHE WANTS TO PROFIT FROM HER OWN ERRORS
SHE WANTS TO BE A PERSON OF HONESTY AND GOOD FAITH
SHE WANTS TO MAKE HER "MARK" IN LIFE

WHAT KIND OF NUT IS SHE?

About the Authors

Judith and Allan Smith have been in Home Based Businesses for over twenty years. Judy owned and operated her own retail fabric store and has taught sewing classes. She is a professional Architectural Modelmaker and a licensed Interior Decorator. She and Allan originated National Doll Society of America and publish Dollsense Newsletter. Allan has written and taught classes and seminars on Home-based businesses. He is an author and publisher, the latest books are Teenage Money Making Guide, How to Make School Fun and How to Market Your Home Made Products. They live on a small ranch near West Palm Beach Florida with their five children.

He distributes other authored how-to and craft books.

Dedication

This book is dedicated to our Mothers Dorothy Robbins and Vera H. Smith, without them we would not have the love and understanding to produce this publication.

TABLE OF CONTENTS

PREFACE

If you can sew and have a sewing machine you have a potential money-making business right in your home. Most people only use 10% of their talent and hidden abilities. If you have this talent you have an advantage over many others.

Don't be afraid of starting small, you have only one way to go and that is up!

Don't get discouraged at first. You'll find hurdles and problems, but none that can not be overcome with the right attitude and persistence. Think of any mistakes as a learning process. Talk over your plans with people who can help and encourage you. In this book we will try to cover a lot of the basics that many forget or avoid when starting out on their own. Many of these suggestions you already know. What we want to do is to give you a plan or guide that will make it easier for you to achieve success and satisfaction from your efforts.

When undertaking any project or goal the first thing we have to have is "Desire" to accomplish a particular goal. You may want to work on one or two specific items such as doll clothes or you may want to design and create women's fashion clothes. Whatever you do, develop a BURNING DESIRE to be successful.

The second thing that would be helpful is to have the right attitude. Be prepared for setbacks and problems as well as successes.

TRACHSLER
© "SEWING FOR PROFIT"

"I NEED 20 OF THESE BY NEXT THURSDAY!"

The third important quality is to have persistence. Don't give up right away; try again. You may be just on the verge of success. Dr. Robert Schuler (Pastor of the Crystal Cathedral in California) had a woman on his Sunday TV program who was divorced, lived in Hawaii and was practically penniless. She was dissatisfied with the Mu Mus in the local stores and decided to use the talent she had. She sewed one that she thought was right. A friend asked her to make one for her, then another friend. One thing led to another and within a year she was producing 123 Mu Mus a week. IMAGINE! In the Mu Mu capital of the world! How much more competition could there be? See what talent, desire, persistence and the right attitude can do. YOU are just as talented as she is. YOU can be successful also! Our biggest hurdle is ourselves.

A fourth asset is to be able to sew well. Do you need to brush up on some aspects of your abilities? Ask another accomplished sewer for advice. Take a course at your local Adult Education School. We humans are just like a green plant, either growing or dying. Are you improving or just resting on your laurels? The local schools' evening classes cost very little and usually run one night a week from 8 to 10 weeks long. Subscribe to trade magazines or pick some up at your newsstand. Join organizations which will give you more exposure. It could be from the school P.T.A., Chamber of Commerce, Senior Citizens groups, church organizations, etc.

As Executive Secretary of the National Doll Society of America, Judy has received numerous samples of doll clothes hand sewn. You couldn't buy this quality anywhere. Many of our members make a good dollar at this type of sewing.

Visit ALL the fabric stores and ask questions and buy a little bit from each one. The more you circulate the more people will know you and the more information you will be exposed to. It is pretty hard to remain an island in this ever-shrinking world.

Discouragement is your worst enemy, and it can creep up on you when you least expect it. Be ready for it. It is a way of telling you that you must work harder if you are going to succeed. GET UP! GET READY! GET OUT OF THE HOUSE AND DO IT! IT WON'T COME TO YOU! START NOW!!

The business world is made up of Winners and Losers. You and only you will determine into which category you will fit. As in any sport or music, it is the person with determination and persistence who stars on the team or becomes part of an orchestra. Fortunately for the Winners there are very few of them and a lot of Losers who usually stand around with each other and ask, "What happened?"

If you want to make money, there are basic rules and principles you must follow. When you compete for the dollar there are a lot of sharp, experienced people ahead of you, which means that it takes a determined, well-organized and persistent person to compete and WIN!!!

You have many advantages going for you. First, your independence will allow you to work longer and with more vigor. Second, you will be able to work for less compensation as you are growing. Most companies have overhead (expenses) that you don't. Third, by working for less monies at first you can take on areas that your competition cannot (competition as the better established and larger businesses). Very few, I repeat, very few people seem to be able to compete with successful businesses. That is why the world is open to you . . . if you want to work harder and smarter.

In the following chapters we will give you the tools and information to be a SUCCESSFUL WINNER . . . but you need the right attitude and want. We would advise those who take this advice as a lot of garbage, to gently lay down this book and go watch TV with the rest of the Losers!!!!

Judy & Allan Smith

CHAPTER 1
IS GOING INTO BUSINESS
FOR YOU?

Many people have talents in this world. But the real test of the talent is the ability to market or sell the results of this talent, art or skill.

A. QUESTIONS TO ASK YOURSELF

There are many questions you must ask yourself before you make the final decision to "go into business."

1. Is the product I produce wanted by enough people to justify the time and expense of going into business? You may want to make Mu Mus in Alaska or knit mittens in Miami. These are great products but if you make them you may have to sell them somewhere else.

2. If you do decide to knit mittens in Miami, do you realize that you may have to market (promote, advertise, sell) them somewhere else OR advertise in a magazine or paper that people with cold hands read?

3. If you have the product and an area that will buy them, is the product well-made and durable? You will have to let others give you constructive advice on this.

4. Can you make the product and sell it profitably? We know of many people who hand make, paint, sculpture, mold etc. items, sell them and end up with about 13 cents per hour in profit. To be successful you must be able to produce the product in a time frame that will pay you over starvation wages.

5. Do you have enough skill or time to produce or sew a large quantity? Some people have made a superior product, advertised or run an article in a magazine and found the results so successful that they could not make enough to satisfy the demands in a reasonable amount of time. Think . . . if you get an order for 50 mittens tomorrow, how long will it take to produce? If you had an order for 100 doll dresses from a wholesaler what would you do?

6. Will you BURN OUT? If you are on the 200th red doll dress with white trim, will you end up in the "SEWER'S PSYCHO WARD"?

7. Do you have a place where you can work without interruption and privacy? It's pretty hard to set up the machine among the usual family confusion without having coffee stains on the material or mistakenly sewing a button on your little poodle.

8. Do you have the encouragement and support of your spouse or others who share you abode? You must demand respect and be allowed to pursue your project. (Read GETTING YOUR FAMILY INTERESTED AND EXCITED IN YOUR PROJECT).

9. Do you have the financial resources to give your business a fair start? The BIGGEST cause of failure in small businesses today is the lack of start-up and sustaining funds (See charter on GETTING, BUDGETING, SPENDING AND KEEPING MONEY). Enthusiasm is great! But this alone will not make a business successful. It's like a lot of young people who think that all their problems will be solved when they get married. Love will conquer all, except empty stomachs, rent, taxes, clothes, gas, etc. etc. The enthusiasm soon dwindles after reality sets in.

10. Remember that as we talk about hurdles and pitfalls, we have to assume that many people are SUCCESSFUL in their attempts. Are you ready for instant success? Oh, sure we all have places and things to spend the monies on, but are we willing to sacrifice and work even harder when the flood gates open? Sometimes it takes more capital and time to expand and meet demands. It could mean time away from your family, friends, or social demands. Will you make sacrifices?

11. Do you have the basic knowledge of bookkeeping, how to handle accounts payable, accounts receivable, balance sheets,

profit and loss statements, debits and credits? You don't have to know all about them, BUT you MUST know how to handle money.

If your answers are YES to most of these questions, then read on, you've got the right attitude and enthusiasm for business!

B. YOUR SUCCESSES

Are you totally satisfied with the progress you have made so far in life? You have many accomplishments to be proud of. You may have raised children, gone through a successful marriage, graduated from high school or college, worked at a job for so many years and done well. BUT nothing, and I repeat, nothing beats being in business for yourself and the feeling of creating and having others accept your own creation.

Before thinking about going into business for ourselves let's put our life into perspective. A positive attitude — to be a success, we have to first believe we are going to be successful! Many of us have undertaken projects or businesses before and they have not become winners. SO WHAT! Some of the most successful people in the world have failed many times. This is all in the past. We can't do anything about yesterday. LEARN FROM YESTERDAY. LIVE FOR TODAY AND PLAN FOR TOMORROW. Let's take a look at our accomplishments so far. Write in the following spaces at least 10 of **your** successes. They will be easy to list as **all** of us have had successes. Learning a skill, taking a course, raising children, driving a car, creating a relationship and friendships, etc.

MY SUCCESSES SO FAR IN LIFE

1.
2.
3.
4.
5.
6.
7.
8.
9.
10.

Quite a list, isn't it!

As your enthusiasm grows for this venture into Sewing for Profits, you may find some who will try to talk you out of it. Some will say it will never work. If you have done your homework, preparation and believe in the project DON'T let anyone discourage you. A lot will be envious and want other failures like themselves.

7

I repeat, make sure you have done thorough preparation and then make the final decision. You might read this book and decide it is too much work. Then that will be a success. Knowing that you cannot do a certain thing is not a failure, it's just avoiding a failure.

Allan thought he could fly a plane. He took lessons, entered flight school and finally soloed. On one landing he was watching the altimeter and not the ground and found the plane dusting the treetops that preceded the runway. It was a close call, but it was a lesson and a success. He climbed out of the cockpit and had a good talk with himself. He decided it would be bad if he took his life in an accident, but what if he had one of our five children riding along. He realized that he was too impulsive to be a good careful pilot. To be a good pilot you must be very exact and careful. He decided he would not qualify, walked away from that Cessna 150 and never flew again. We don't have to make everything in life a success; we can't do all things and be all things to all people.

C. STARTING A NEW BUSINESS STATISTICS

According to the Small Business Administration, there are more than 13 million small businesses in America. This represents 97% of the total nation's businesses. They employ 85% of the work force and have an average of five (5) or less employees.

A lot of people start a business as **dreamers,** not as **a person with a plan.** Being enthusiastic and motivated is not enough in today's competitive world.

27% of all small businesses fail in 3 years or less
55% of all small businesses fail in 5 years or less
92% of all small businesses fail in 10 years or less.
(from Dun & Bradstreet's Business Failure Record)

D. WHY DO BUSINESSES FAIL

1. **Poor management.** That does not mean you have to be a student of management, an MBA or an experienced business person. It means that when money making is involved, certain basic business and management skills are needed.

2. **Under-capitalized.** Yep, that means not enough money. Make sure you read the chapter on GETTING, BUDGETING, SPENDING AND KEEPING MONEY.

3. **Lack of product knowledge or skill.** I just picked up some meat at the corner butcher. A new couple had bought the business two days ago and waited on us. Judy asked for some sweetbreads, they looked at us for a while, then pointed to the rack of baked goods and said we could probably find it there. After explaining the error to the new owner, Judy asked him about his

experience in the meat business. He had never had any. He delivered beer to butcher shops and felt he could run the meat business easily.

We Americans have a great "ITCH" to be in business for ourselves. We take all kinds of chances; many times we come out winners. Unfortunately the statistics show that only 8% make it after 10 years. DO WHAT YOU DO BEST, FIND A NEED AND FILL IT. These are the most important words we have heard in a long time. If you sew well and like to do it and can find someone to buy your creation then you have the basics to be a success.

4. **Failure to watch the money flow correctly.** Some businesspeople think that the money coming in is "instant cash" to spend. We must realize that many people are waiting for this money before it is ours. The supply source, phone company, electric company and the government's itchy hands are outstretched and waiting. Depending on how far you want to go with your sewing business will determine how long you can go without taking out any money. Most businesses will not allow you to take out any money for at least six months.

5. **Lack of professional help.** We must have the input of attorneys, accountants, insurance agents, advertising, marketing, mail order, postal and supply people.

6. **Failure to realize the details in the business world.** Many of us are talented and think we can sell our product. We must know how to market our product or service. How many unpublished songs, unwritten books, and undiscovered talents lay dormant. How many good books, songs, inventions and crafts are never created. WE can invent the perfect mousetrap or cure for the common cold, but unless we let others know about it, it will just remain a secret. To be successful selling our product we must know basic business principles. We will try real hard to show you how in this book.

7. **Choosing the wrong business structure.** Should you do it by yourself, with another person (or two) or incorporate? These questions will be important as you become more successful and your product becomes accepted. (Examine the chapter on EXPANDING AND DIVERSIFYING.)

8. **Unable to handle success.** Sound kinda funny? Here are some reasons that might make sense.

    1. **Unable to meet the demands.** I know of a gal who produced cheesecakes in her home. All she made she sold. One day she landed a large restaurant's cheesecake business. Her kitchen and appliances

9

were not large enough to handle the amount they wanted, as a result she lost the account and grew discouraged. The other side of not enough business is too much. Always be prepared for the day you become ultra-successful.

2. **Spending more time spending the money than paying attention to business.** Some small businesses have this happen. They are not accustomed to sudden amounts of large money. Many want to gather the material things they have waited for all these years and forget the basic business.

3. **Hiring more people and overloading the expenses.** This happens to keep up with the demand and the cost of adding people amounts to more than the profit we make.

4. **Not filling orders fast enough.**

5. **Falling down on quality to meet the demands of quantity.**

6. **Taking on other projects and spreading ourselves thin.**

9. **Getting bored with what we are doing.** We may get very tired sewing that 785th apron even though we have orders for another 500.

10. **Getting friction from other family members.** (Read chapter on HOW TO GET OUR FAMILY EXCITED ABOUT OUR PROJECT.)

11. **Unable to meet the demands of increased business.** We can't produce enough from where we are and are unable to find another location or locations.

12. **Letting competition or trusted ones "STEAL" the business.** That world outside our kitchen door is full of people who will take our "eye-teeth" if given a chance. There are a lot of "ME-TOOS" waiting to copy a successful product, book or idea. You will have to protect your product or service by using legal means (copyrights, trade-marks or patents). Also keeping our mouth closed and not letting others know too much about our business or successes.

It has been found that the person who will steal from you is the one who has been with you the longest and has been given the most trust. Any time someone else handles your money, watch! Some of it will probably be gone. We have seen many small business and craft people entrust others to help or advise them and have that trusted soul go out and copy the same thing. Just be careful. This doesn't mean you have to be a skeptic on everything — or everyone — 'nuf said.

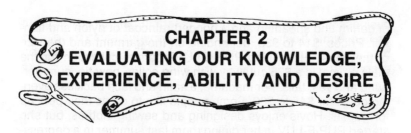

CHAPTER 2
EVALUATING OUR KNOWLEDGE, EXPERIENCE, ABILITY AND DESIRE

In the last chapter we asked ourselves if going into business was our cup of tea. Now we have to explore even further and see if what we have is enough.

A. FINDING OUT MORE ABOUT OURSELF

1. Do I have the skill to produce a quality product? A good way to find this out is to ask friends. You can also discover how well accepted the product is by renting a booth at a small church or town fair. With very little investment you can get a "feel" of the consumer's tastes.

2. Do I have the correct ATTITUDE AND ENTHUSIASM to push me over the top? Sometimes your past performances will answer this.

3. Do I have the physical strength to work long and hard hours until or as the orders come rolling in?

4. Do I have a basic knowledge of the business world? Or do I have a spouse or relative who will guide me along?

SUCCESS STORY from *Money Magazine*

Marjorie Hovis, 43, has made a successful business in selling outrageous dapper dog wear. She offers a western-style coat

of denim and shearling and a hooded raincoat of nylon and flannel. Prices: $14 to $35, depending on the garment and the size of the beast. Headlining PUP-E-LUV's formal collection for the male animal is a $75 cutaway with wing collar, bow-tie, cummerbund and yes, tails. For madame, a satin and lace backless evening gown for $45 to $60. Some people like to dress their pets up for guests. Hovis enjoys designing and sewing clothes, but she started PUP-E-LUV in her dining room last summer in a depressed area to make money. Last February they sold 2000 garments to Neiman-Marcus in San Francisco and the Fred Meyer chain in Oregon and Washington. Her latest creation: a bib for big dogs. "You know," she says, "the big ones that have a slobbering problem."

5. Do I have persistence. Winners are people who will keep trying even when it looks like everything and everybody is against you. After the star of success has landed on you, many people will say, "Oh, sure she was LUCKY!" Let's look into this word LUCK, if there is such a word or do we make our own LUCK?

1. Many lucky people are extroverts; they have magnetic personalities. They communicate well with their voices, eyes, facial expressions, poise and manners. If we have a negative communication field, we can do something about it.

2. Get in touch with your feelings. Lucky people have an ability to "feel" their way through life. They trust their "gut" feelings and usually make the right decisions the rest of the time.

3. Do your homework. Lucky people are not lazy. They gather facts, analyze them and make decisions the rest of the time.

4. Recognize an opportunity when it comes along. They drift by every day, but do we always see them? And even if we do, do we take action on them at once?

5. Take risks — Lucky people are bold people. They are willing to do something a little unorthodox if the possibility of success is there. Stubborn people are usually lucky people. They refuse to give up.

6. Know when to quit while you are far ahead.

7. Admit your mistakes. Can you say "I was wrong!" and then to proceed to rectify the error?

(Source: *UPWARD MOBILITY,* by Catalyst. Holt, Rinehart Publishers, N.Y.)

SUCCESS STORY
Mary Hudson borrowed $400 and opened a gasoline service station. Twenty years later she owns hundreds of them throughout the country and is a multimillionaire.

Actress Ellen Burstyn says being successful in her 40s has changed her life and made it more exciting. Recently she pulled into a garage to collect her car and, with some concern, rubbed what she thought was a chip in the paint. A man standing by saw this and remarked, "You had better hope it's NOT a dent, or HE won't let YOU in the house tonight!" Burstyn drew on years of self discipline to stop from haughtily replying and said, "I bought this car and no man can keep me out of my house . . . because I bought that too!"

ANOTHER SUCCESS FORMULA
1. Work for yourself . . . the real money is in entrepreneur-ship, like YOU and YOUR product(s).

2. Do something you like . . . long hours and hard work is fun when you enjoy it!

3. NEVER STOP LEARNING or specializing in your field.

4. Find a need and fill it!

5. Research your subject thoroughly, try to know as much as is known on the subject.

6. Experiment with new approaches; if one door is closed, try another.

7. Recognize a lucky break when it comes along and USE IT!

8. Expect to work long hours and make sacrifices!

9. Recognize a failure early and pull out; sacrifice pride and sentiment!

10. Publicize your success; make others believe the credit is yours.

11. Don't let making money be your prime source of motivation!

B. YOU MAY HAVE MORE TALENT THAN YOU THOUGHT
In the following categories list a talent, expertise or experience you have had in life. Don't say, "Oh, I can't do anything too well." HOG WASH! Have you taught your kids to tie a shoelace, read, eat? Have you made a presentation to a group? Have you sewed a sweater or knitted a pair of mittens, crocheted an afghan? Have you graduated from high school, taken other courses, learned to

14

play an instrument, planted a garden, milked a cow, driven a tractor or mower? Have you cut the kids' or dogs' hair, balanced the checkbook, learned to type, worked a computer, bandaged a bad cut? Have you written a poem or short story, got a loan from the bank, made a sign, drawn a picture, cooked a meal, started a stalled car,? Then met an important person!!

EDUCATION (formal, correspondence, informal)
1.
2.
3.

MECHANICAL SKILLS (motors, appliances, carpentry, plumbing, etc.)
1.
2.
3.

CRAFT/HOBBY SKILLS (crafts, music, writing)
1.
2.
3.

PHYSICAL (sports, exercise, strength, etc.)
1.
2.
3.

BUSINESS (typing, balancing checkbook, bookkeeping, cash registers, etc.)
1.
2.
3.

ORGANIZATIONAL (officer of club, originated an organization, member of committee, gave report, gave talk)
1.
2.
3.

PERSONAL (smile, personality, figure, looks, etc.)
1.
2.
3.

HUMAN RELATIONS (friendly, dependable, honest, sincere, sensitive, etc.)
1.
2.
3.

COMMUNITY INVOLVEMENT (charity, political, religious, school, local government, etc.)
1.
2.
3.

FAMILY (I'm a good daughter, sister, mother. I have the respect of ----)
1.
2.
3.

Now, See what you are, a talented person with a lot of qualities.

C. DON'T QUIT

When things go wrong, as they sometimes will,
When the road you're trudging seems all uphill,
When the funds are low and the debts are high,
And you want to smile, but you have to sigh,
When care is pressing you down a bit —
Rest if you must, but don't you quit.
Life is queer with its twists and turns,
As every one of us sometimes learns,
And many a fellow turns about
When he might have won had he stuck it out.
Don't give up though the pace seems slow —
You may succeed with another blow.
Often the goal is nearer than it seems to a faint and faltering man;
Often the struggler has given up
When he might have captured the victor's cup;
And he learned too late when the night came down,
How close he was to the golden crown.
Success is failure turned inside out —
The silver tint of the clouds of doubt,
And you never can tell how close you are,
It may be near when it seems afar;
So stick to the fight when you're hardest hit —
It's when things seem worst that you mustn't quit.

Author Unknown

D. WHY DO PEOPLE GO INTO SEWING RETAILING

There are three basic reasons to go into sewing retailing.

1. Some people go in to provide themselves with a job.

2. Some have a pre-determined standard of living and see sewing as a way to earn enough money to maintain this standard.

3. Owners of the business are seeking an adequate return

for both time and money. Successful craft sewing people belong to this group. They take a cold analysis and expect an adequate return for every dollar invested. They also try to keep their money working. They place a value on their time. The more money you have to start up the greater chance of your success.

SUCCESS STORY

As a young gal, she worked for a party-plan cosmetic company. She didn't like the treatment she was getting so she started her own company. A small proprietary manufacturer supplied her with a private line of cosmetics. Soon she became so successful she bought out this manufacturer. In 1976 her company was listed on the New York Stock Exchange; her name . . . of course, Mary Kay Ash.

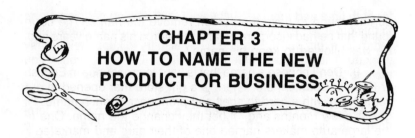

CHAPTER 3
HOW TO NAME THE NEW
PRODUCT OR BUSINESS

1. It should be original.

2. It should be easy to pronounce.

3. Can it be easily remembered and recognized?

4. It should describe the product or business's outstanding benefits.

5. It should not have negative connotations.

6. Test it out on friends and relatives. Notice their responses.

7. Have a logo or a drawing to place on calling cards, stationery, price tags, order forms, etc.

8. If you are going to incorporate then you will have to submit the name(s) to the State. You will have to have a second and third choice in case the name is being used by another.

When the Ed Sullivan Show was popular they had the name protected and would not allow anyone else to use it. It seems that there was a small TV store called Ed Sullivan TV. The big cor-

poration sued to have the person remove the name. The court found that he had incorporated and registered his name years ago. He was allowed to keep his name.

9. Don't choose a name that is hard to pronounce in English or French, Spanish, etc. There is a gift store that opened in our home town with a hard to spell and pronounce French name. I'll give it a few months and I'll bet they change the name. One of the large auto makers named one of their cars and marketed it in Spanish countries. They didn't realize, until it was too late, that it was a slang word to Spanish people. They had a tough time selling those cars in the Latin countries.

CHAPTER 4
ESTABLISHING A PLAN

Every goal or procedure may not be accomplished **BUT** it is a road or a direction to travel. Let's show you what we mean in this example.

Linda Gray is a creator of soft dolls. Her husband's name is Joe. She makes the body, stuffs them, outlines the contours of the body, paints the face, knits the hair and either buys the clothes or sews them. She has a saleable market. Her plan of action is:

Project	To be done by	Cost	By whom done
1. Create a name	May 1	—	Linda
2. Determine price	May 1	—	Linda
3. Determine time to make ..	May 1	—	Linda
4. Find and list suppliers	May 6	—	Linda
5. Order supplies (for 12)....	May 6	37.50	Linda
6. Outline a budget.........	May 6	—	Linda/Joe
7. Obtain d/b/a name	May 10	5.00	Joe
8. Open a bank account	May 10	200.00	Linda
9. Order cloth labels........	May 12	20.00	Linda
10. Check on insurance	May 12	—	Joe

11. Buy bookkeeping paper . . .	May 15	15.00	Joe
12. Check & oil sewing machine	May 15	—	Joe
13. Set up work area	May 15	—	Linda/Joe
14. Finish first 3 bodies	May 20	—	Linda
15. Establish marketing plan . .	May 20	—	Linda/Joe
16. Advertise & test	May 23	55.00	Linda
17. Place on consignment	May 23	—	Linda
18. Finish next three	May 23	—	Linda
19. Etc., etc., etc.			

See how easily things will fall into place if you have a plan to follow. The plan must be flexible to change. The thrill of seeing this procedure completed is great in itself.

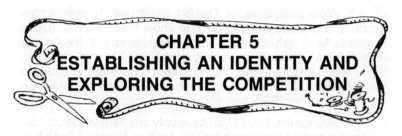

CHAPTER 5
ESTABLISHING AN IDENTITY AND EXPLORING THE COMPETITION

We will assume that your product or service will be ultra-successful and that your identity will be well known. What do we do to prepare for this day?

1. You must give quality or quantity. Do you want to offer more than your competition? If you want to give more for the money or a better product, you should decide now. Your entrance into the business work leaves impressions with many people. You want it to be the best!

2. Have a name, either for your business or for your product. Ever hear of the Pet-Rock or the Cabbage Patch Kids? How about the Apple computer? ALL of these started in the home or garage. If you decide on Elma's Notions or Vera's Sewing, have a name.

3. Have some calling cards or a small inexpensive slinger brochure made up. You can have 500 calling cards made up for around $10.00.

4. Your address. Some advocate renting a post office box. In all of our experience, we have found that your authenticity is better if you use your home address.

5. Your bank account. This is a tough one. To open a bank account in most banks you have to show them a d.b.a. (Doing Business As . . . which means you are registered with the County) or give them a financial statement. Who has a financial statement if you are just starting out. You will need a business account for many reasons. One of the most important reasons will be for Uncle Sam and the IRS when you become successful.

6. A price list. Even if you have only one item you must have a price list stating how much for one, for five, twenty, or one hundred. I'm sure you will give a discount for more than 4 or 6 units. Make sure you have all discounts and payable info on this list.

7. Have a goal or a procedure. Even if you write with lipstick on a piece of tissue, you must have a direction. Where would a sailboat be without a rudder? It would go where the winds or current wants it to go. You are the same; you must have a direction or plan.

EXPLORING THE COMPETITION
After you have determined which business you are going into, it would be advisable to explore the competition:

1. How many others are in the same area you want to cover? You may find very few or none.

2. What are they charging? Write it down and compare.

3. What do they give for what they charge? Ultra-successful business always give more in quantity or quality than their competitors. Ray Kroc (Mr. McDonald's) found a way to give a quality hamburger at a very low cost. John Y. Brown (Mr. Kentucky Fried Chicken) found a way to give **quality** chicken to the consumer at a moderate, economical, price. People Express Airline cut fares in half, reduced expense and is now beating the giants in the very difficult airline business.

4. What is their reputation among the public? If you find they have a moderate or poor image, then you will have an advantage.

Gather all this competitive knowledge and determine what you will charge, what you will give, what area you will concentrate on and what image you want to have. Many successful entrepreneurs (businesspeople) find when they enter a new market area (business area) that the best way to get the competitors' customers over to them is to:

1. **Undercut their price.** Gas stations are famous for this when opening a new location. The large supermarket completely eliminated the corner Ma and Pa grocery store by giving food items at lower prices. They found that the consumer (customer) will

sacrifice service (clerks, deliveries, charge accounts, etc.) for low prices. You should determine what is most important in the business you are starting.

2. **Give them more for their money.** 7-11 officials say that their biggest volume and most profitable item is the "Big Gulp" soft drink. They said pooey to Burger King and McDonald's and gave twice as much for 59 cents.

3. **What area do they cover?** If it is a big, well organized, "Winner" type business, stay away from their area. It will take too much money, effort and time to compete. Either cover another area or change your business. Successful independent fabric stores will not open near Jo-Ann Fabrics. You will have enough problems; try to eliminate as many as possible BEFORE you start.

If you decide not to give more in quantity, in other words you want to maintain the same price or even higher than others, you **MUST** be able to improve the quality of your services or goods. When we start out in business we must attract the customer to us. Just because you sell or produce a need for a particular thing with enthusiasm, a smile and a lot of desires, does not guarantee the public will tear down your doors to give you money. You **MUST** give something that will attract them to buy, to send their friends and to come back again. There are many Quick Printers in the business. Observe the differences in quality of the finished product. Go to a recognized restaurant, order their $4.95 Hamburg (they call it chopped sirloin) and compare it with a McDonald's. Have your film developed at certain drugstores. They offer two prints for the price of one and the option to return unwanted prints. (The end product, developed film, is the same anywhere, but they offer you freebies.)

4. **What is your competition's reputation?** This will be a good indication of how tough your fight will be. Usually the longer someone is in business the better established they are and the more accepted they are to the general public. What do you recognize first, Radio Shack or Bruce's Electronics? This is another incentive to try harder. Remember Avis Car Rental slogan, "We are not number one, but we try harder!" When Allan was in business he changed it and used it as . . . "We are Number One and Still Try Harder!"

In reverse, if your competition has a poor reputation . . . bad or inferior products or service, rude or disinterested service personnel, undependable, high prices, sloppy work, dirty premises or people, etc. etc. . . . . **THEN** it's your turn to take away their customers and attract those who will not go there. How many times have you called a TV, electrician, air conditioning/heating type company and they never show up or are two days late? A great majority of small businesses have this problem.

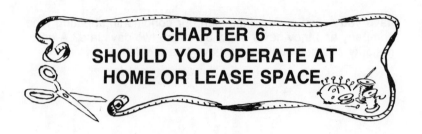

CHAPTER 6
SHOULD YOU OPERATE AT
HOME OR LEASE SPACE

Whether you are starting out or already established, the question of where to operate your business always comes up.

A. QUESTIONS TO ASK YOURSELF

1. Can I function effectively at home?

2. Do I depend on walk-in or passing-by traffic?

3. Do I live near a suitable location?

4. Can I afford to move the business out of my home?

5. Can I afford the time away from family?

6. Will the sale of my products pay for the overhead?

7. Will this move increase my effectiveness and increase the sale of my product(s)?

8. Do I have multiple products that will appeal to the customers?

B. ADVANTAGES OF HAVING AN OUTSIDE SHOP
1. Privacy (you can lock the door and be alone)

2. Exposure to more potential customers

3. Security from other family members (kids etc. taking supplies and tools)

4. Room to display goods

5. Potential of having others share expenses and displaying their creations

6. Free from neighbors and zoning restrictions

7. Absence of interruptions from family

8. Far away from refrigerator

9. Authentic address

C. ADVANTAGES OF KEEPING THE BUSINESS AT HOME
1. Travel time eliminated

2. Rent expenses eliminated

3. Electricity etc. furnished at no extra charge (unless you have converted a garage, cellar, attic, barn or added a room)

4. If you have to parent or child-sit, you can combine both

5. You can eat lunch, have coffee etc. with family

6. You can watch the premises and secure it against trespassers

7. You can be informal in dress etc.

8. You can start with the family phone

9. If you want to "goof off" it is easier

10. The refrigerator is closer

11. Sewing machines etc. don't have to be lugged back and forth or duplicated

D. IF YOU DECIDE TO OPEN A SHOP OR STORE
Let's check and see if you are ready for this big decision to open your store.

1. I have enough funds to last (pay expenses) for six months, NOT including owner's profit OR salary.

2. I have enough to pay for the cost of the lease. If your rent is $300 per month and you have a year lease then you have an obligation of $3600.

3. I have the ability and the resources to decorate and merchandise the store.

4. I have decided on the hours, signage, name etc.

5. I have a lease that I can live with.

6. I realize the FIRST THREE IMPORTANT RULES of finding a place is:

    1.   LOCATION!
    2.   LOCATION!
    3.   LOCATION!

7. I realize the amount of TIME I must spend to make this a success.

8. My family realizes the sacrifices I will have to make.

9. It is within a few minutes of home.

10. It is in a relatively SAFE neighborhood.

NOW LET'S LIST SOME STEPS THAT WILL HELP MAKE THE OPENING EASIER.

1. The location is the best possible.

2. I have a lease that has been examined by an authority.

3. The premises have sufficient:

    a. Heat

    b. Air conditioning

    c. Bathrooms

    d. Exits

    e. Electrical outlets

    f. Security (doors, local police, etc.)

    g. Lighting

    h. Exposure to passers-by

    i. Outside maintenance (snow removal, electrical, sidewalks, etc.

    j. Customer AND employee parking

    k. Traffic — we mean walking by of potential customers

    l. Floors, ceilings and walls. Don't laugh, if you go into a new mall or plaza store they give you only a structure. You have to put in your own ceilings, floors, plumbing, heating, etc.

m. Landlord insurance to cover the structural and premise liability

4. The landlord will give me enough time to get ready. Many times they give an extra month to repaint, re-tile floors, etc. Especially if you are IMPROVING their property.

5. I have the talent or a person(s) to help me redecorate, move, clean-up and set-up.

6. Have a list of necessities to open the door:

Display show cases
Wall and gondola racks
Display racks
Electrical (lighting, etc.)
Cash box or register
Sewing machine
Typewriter, photocopying machine
Adding machine/calculator
Change (money)
Bookkeeping materials
Radio, tape player
Uniforms, name tags, or aprons
Bathroom needs
Vacuum, mop, etc.

Wrapping materials
Bags, tape, string, labels
Receipt books
Master/Visa equipment
Bank deposit materials
Bank account & check book
Locks and keys
Telephone
Desk, filing cabinet
Business cards, stationery
Signs, inside and out
Small refrigerator
Cleaning materials
etc. etc.

7. Make out an Emergency Chart:

Electrician . . . . Jones 622-1234
Plumber . . . . Brown 722-2345
Heating — A/C . . . . Green 822-1234
Police 222-1111
Fire 111-2222
Water Department 333-2255
Power Company 444-3456
Telephone Repair 345-7890
Rescue Squad 234-6789
Landlord . . . . J. Grey 135-9001
My Home Phone . . . . A. Smith 234-1212
Office Equipment Repair . . . . ABC Co. 234-6665
Office Supplies . . . . ABC Co. 234-6665
etc.

ELECTRICAL BOX . . . . located to the right of bathroom
WATER METER & SHUT OFF . . . . located outside rear entrance
AIR CONDITION/HEAT . . . . . Located in basement on NE wall
STORE LIGHT SWITCHES . . . . to right of front entrance

OIL/GAS TANK AND REFILL VALVE .....in basement in SE corner, valves outside bathroom
CLEANING EQUIPMENT ....in bathroom under sink
FUSES, LIGHT BULBS...........in equipment cabinet next to bathroom
FIRE EXTINGUISHER...................outside bathroom
FIRST AID KIT......................in equipment cabinet
etc. etc.

8. Have a procedure plan and schedule. (You are probably wondering WHY all these details if you are going to be the only one to run the shop. You may need a day off, an hour off. You may hire part-time or full time help . . . OR you may forget.) The little time that these procedures take, will more than pay for itself. It will help you think and operate in a business-like manner . . . to become ORGANIZED and EFFICIENT.

BUSINESS HOURS .... M-T-W-Th-F 9:00-6:00
Sat. 9:00-1:00

DISCOUNT SCHEDULE
Senior Citizens 10%
Employees...25%
Other merchants....................................10%
Police, clergy 10%

PAYMENTS
Rent ....first of month
Phone...................................10th of month
Electric.................................10th of month
Water, etc...............................10th of month
Payables ....10th of month
Loan ....5th of month
etc. etc.

9. NOW have an idea of WHAT you are going to stock the shelves with, the amount and variety of goods and WHERE you will obtain them and HOW MUCH they will cost (refer to your budget). Start an inventory control system.

    a. Alphabetize the inventory according to company or product. If you order from just a few suppliers it would be advisable to list just the products.

    b. The advantages of keeping good inventory records outweigh the trouble and time it takes.

        1) You have tighter control on your purchases.

        2) You can estimate profits easier.

3) There is proof in case of fire or theft.

4) Pilferage, internal and external can be detected.

5) Any questions from tax authorities can be substantiated.

6)"Winners" and "Dog" merchandise are immediately spotted.

   c.   You can use 3x5 cards, one for each product. Obviously each button or spool of thread cannot be inventoried. This method would be great for businesses with small inventories.

   d.   Don't make it too detailed or complicated as it may discourage proper utilization.

   e.   For larger businesses we recommend more detailed information such as:
Date of Purchase
Amount of Initial Order
Cost, Mark-up and Retail
Reorder Information
Etc.
Many sewing retailers use home and business computers to store inventory data. There are many excellent soft-ware programs available.

10. Display your goods. Now you can do some creative displaying and decorating to make the merchandise appealing to the consumer. Don't just stock the items. MAKE THEM ATTRACTIVE and IRRESISTABLE!!!

CHAPTER 7
OBTAINING START-UP MONEY,
BUDGETING AND SIMPLE BOOKKEEPING

The two biggest reasons businesses fail are poor managerial expertise and low capitalization. In other words, being a poor business person and not knowing how to correctly spend money. If you follow the procedures in this chapter, you will have good managerial direction and know how to budget and FIND start up money. Whether you are producing one dress a month or 50 blouses a week, you still will need a plan, a direction, a BUDGET.

A. FINDING OUT WHAT YOU NEED

Before we discuss budgets let's find out how much we need, IF we need it and WHAT we need.

Let's make some lists:

1. Itemize EVERYTHING you need to produce your creation(s) — from paper clips, needles to typewriters, sewing machine and computers. Spend some time thinking and list everything you will need to produce the QUALITY and QUANTITY of what you will make and sell. Packing materials, postage, labels, fabric, fillings, ribbons, thread, etc. etc.

2. Go over the list and list the ESSENTIALS only — only the items that will bring INSTANT CASH to your business, cross off the rest.

3. Take the essential list and try to acquire, build, borrow or rent without having to finance or buy.

4. Try to borrow as many items on this list as you can. This will not cost you any money. If you borrow from a friend they will become involved and probably lend you a helping hand or a good word.

5. For the remaining items try to rent. Borrowing or renting is sensible. If the business is good then you can buy the item. If the reverse happens you can return the items.

6. If you rent office equipment it is 100% deductible.

B. PRODUCING A BUDGET

After you have borrowed, built, refurbished, and rented everything you can, let's make a list and find out what you still need.

Figure out the amount of material etc. you will need to do six months of business. (Six months will give you a pretty good indication of the way the business is going to go.) You should be able to support yourself in this period of time WITHOUT taking out profit. Don't forget salaries and taxes.

GOT a figure? Again it should be for a six month period of time.

WE have a new idea for a soft doll. Let's see what it will cost to produce it at home.

Refurbish room (attic, garage, barn, cellar, outhouse). IT IS IMPORTANT THAT YOU HAVE YOUR OWN ROOM OR AREA IN WHICH TO CREATE AND WORK!!

Cost to refurbish room or area (mostly done by my husband and material we scrounged)	$ 75.00
Materials for 250 dolls	525.00
Packing materials	25.00
Imprinted labels (500)	55.00
Printing of descriptive brochure (100)	50.00
Office materials	25.00
Printing, calling cards, stationery	50.00
Shipping, postage	30.00
Misc.	100.00
	$935.00
	$935.00

Advertising (newspapers, magazines) six months	$2000.00
Advertising, mailing lists	1500.00
Fees, craft shows, fairs, flea markets	200.00

Display materials for shows etc. 150.00
                                                 ─────────
                                                 $3850.00
                                         Total $4785.00

This means that you will have to have about $5000 to produce 250 dolls over a six month period. Chances are that with the amount of advertising you will do, they will sell out.

If they cost $5000 and you sell 250, that means each cost you $20. MANY OVERLOOK THE ADDED COSTS AND JUST FIGURE THE MATERIAL AND SHIPPING COSTS. You will have to charge $40 to double your money. This is not the ULTIMATE list but it shows you how to determine the cost of what you are selling.

If you do not advertise then your cost will be much less. You could have a cost factor of $3-4 BUT will you sell them? You may attend fairs, crafts shows, flea markets etc. AND you may put them on consignment.

May we repeat IT IS IMPORTANT TO PUT YOUR EXPENSES DOWN ON PAPER THEN DETERMINE WHICH MARKETING ROUTE YOU WILL TAKE!!!

If you sell 500 dolls with the same expenses then you will cut your costs and increase your profit.

If you rent a shop and display your creation(s) let's look at the costs that we will have to ADD ON.

Rent (per month $200) six months $1200
Electricity ($50/month) six months 300
Water, sewer, garbage, etc. ($20/month) $20x6 120
Phone ($50/month) $50x6 300
Insurance per year. $150 (6 months) 75
Additional display cases etc. 500
Misc. 600
                                                 ─────────
                                                   $3095

We have now added over $3000 to the $5000 that we started with. $8000 would mean selling 200 dolls JUST to break even. Obviously you would have more than just a doll in your store.

1. Have others contribute or consign their hand-made items.

2. Buy already-made goods to sell.

3. Sell kits, patterns, materials etc.

4. etc. etc.

What if we don't sell enough dolls or additional items?

1. You have to cut expenses OR increase your price.

2. Add other items to sell along with your doll.

3. Your advertising and promotions are ineffective.

4. You have the wrong product.

5. Your price is wrong.

6. Your timing is wrong.

7. The item is not appealing to the consumer.

We have previously determined that we will need about $8000 to produce our creation in a rented store or $5000 to effectively produce and market the produce from a home base.

C. WHERE TO GET THE MONEY

We have determined we need $5000, and we need it for about 6 months to a year. We should offer, or will be obligated to pay interest. This can be a real bummer. If you are charged 15% per year on the $5000, then you will have to pay back $5750 at the end of the year. The $750 is an expense and will have to be added on the cost of doing business or onto the cost of the product.

1. First look around the house, your relatives' houses, barn, garage, cellar, attic for saleable-nonused items. Have a garage sale or participate in a flea market. You'd be surprised at the amount of things you never use that others will buy from you.

2. Borrow on your life insurance policy.

3. Borrow against your savings. If you are a good customer the bank will lend you YOUR money back for a percent or two interest charge. BUT your money will still be in the bank and will still be earning interest. (If you have $5000 in a saving account paying 10% interest, the bank may lend you $5000 at 11 or 12% interest.)

4. Re-mortgage your home. Get an equity loan.

5. Get a secured loan. This means you have collateral or assets to pledge to the bank in case you cannot or won't pay. President Harry Truman once stated that a bank will lend you money if you can prove you don't need it.

6. Sell your car and lease one through the business.

7. Approach the SBA, Small Business Administration. They have an office in the Federal Building. We have known numerous people who have secured loans this way. You have an advantage if you are a woman. (You must be turned down by three banks first.)

8. Ask your spouse, brother, cousin, mother, grandfather or a friend. Offer to pay the going interest rate, sign a note OR give them a piece of the business. Roy Kroc, the McDonald's owner gave away most of his interest in the business in the beginning. He ended up with less than 20%. He borrowed a small amount from his secretary and gave her some stock. Today she lives in Palm Beach, a millionaire. The stock increased in value that much. If your business is worth $25,000 and you need $5000 then you will have to give away 25%. For every dollar profit the lender will get 25¢ AND STILL have the original $5000 coming back PLUS interest.

9. Form a Board of Advisors and ask them to contribute or lend the company so much money.

D. APPROACHING THE BANK (The last chance)

Realize that a bank will NOT lend you money if you don't have certain items. If you go in and just ask for $5000 to open a business, they will deny you. They will not lend money unless the person has some of their money invested. They could start the business themselves and HIRE YOU to run it. Here are some things you should have.

1. Have an account at the bank where you want to borrow money; a savings account will help a lot, also having your home mortgage there.

2. Have a history of being a good risk. You have paid back previous loans promptly.

3. Have a financial statement prepared. They will give you the necessary forms to fill out.

4. Have a proof of YOUR investment and assets IN the business.

5. Have proof of collateral — a car, a home, stocks, property etc.

6. If you are married, your spouse will have to sign the loan papers also. He/She will be liable for the unpaid amount as you will.

7. Shop around for the best rate(s) especially if you have strong collateral and a good bank reputation.

8. You will pay more interest on an unsecured loan than on a secured loan.

9. Some loans can be paid back on a monthly basis; some can be paid at the end of the loaning time. BUT you will have to pay the interest periodically.

10. Don't ever try to "CON" the bank. Be honest and they will do their best for you.

11. Make friends with a banker OR BETTER YET his/her secretary. They can do you a lot of favors and advise you.

12. Try to get in the habit of doing business with one bank. It will be easier to ask for favors if they know you are a good customer.

THE LAST RESORT . . . a finance company. They will be glad to lend you money at 20-30% interest . . . . and WITH a lot of collateral. Try to stay away from these bandits. Your Master/Visa card charges 18-23% on money you owe OR borrow.

E. SIMPLE BOOKKEEPING

It is imperative to keep **GOOD** records if you want to make money. You have probably been in small business shops, stores and studios and have observed "confusion." They are busy making or selling the product but have no idea how much profit they are making.

1. Let's get started with the budget we established previously. This is a financial guideline; it will show how much can be spent. It must be followed and can be reviewed or revised periodically. It will have to be adjusted as business grows or if business does not grow!

2. Have a place to receive and secure the monies coming in. If you have a cash business then you should have a way to record each sale. (Good money-handling procedures now, will prevent shortages, thefts, embezzlements later).

    a.   A cash drawer with a lock and/or secured to a counter. You can buy these at stationery and hardware stores.

    b.   A sales book, with duplicte numbered pages.

    c.   A cash register with recording tape. (There will be a time when you will have someone else collecting money. You want to make sure **ALL** money is put in **YOUR** money drawer.

    d.   A bank account, bank deposit slips, money bags, Master/Visa credit, sales and deposit slips. (You may have a night deposit bag with keys.)

3. In an office supply store, pick up a book of analysis pads — 50 sheets 11x8½ 12 column.

4. Set up a system. Basically it is how much money is coming in, how much is spent and hopefully there is some left over.

This is called profit BEFORE taxes and any amortization (pay back on loans, principal and interest).

1. Use a monthly system, each column is a month (see enclosure) for daily receipts.

NOTE: Right now you are saying "I'm too small to start something like this," or "I'm not good with figures but I'm good with a needle and thread." My answer Pooey! If you sell one creation a month you are not too small to use a system. This is not the ONLY one to use, but it is a suggestion.

2. Record every expense transaction, every check you write. If you spend CASH, keep every receipt and have a petty cash check. (Save up $10 or 20 worth, write a check for that amount and keep the receipts to coincide with the check.)

3. Divide your expenses into catagories — example:
Utilities (light, heat, water, phone)
Rent (if any)
Insurance
Legal (lawyers etc.)
Materials (thread, fabric etc.)
Mailing/postage (postage, shipping materials, labels, mailing lists).
Dues, subscriptions
Equipment
Interest (on loans)
Miscellaneous

You can vary this to your individual needs. List these categories along the side of the ledger. Some months you may have only a few entries. As you grow, bookkeeping procedures will be already established. At the end of the month just total the columns. At the end of the year, total all the total columns and you have your yearly expenses.

5. Two of your columns can be for the money you take in. One for the money, the second for the taxes. Then at the end of the month just total the columns and you have the total gross sales AND the amount of tax that you have collected. This organized method will allow you to determine the profitability of your business. It will save you accountants' fees as they will find facts much easier. The simpler the system the better control you have.

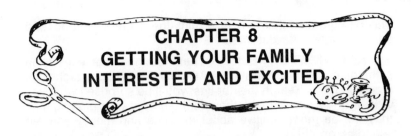

CHAPTER 8
GETTING YOUR FAMILY
INTERESTED AND EXCITED

Your climb to success can be hampered with a spouse, child, or a relative who will not cooperate and give encouragement. One of your preparation procedures should be gaining the support of those to whom you are close.

BE POSITIVE . . . Talk about your successes, hopes and aspirations, not the pitfalls, hurdles or problems that occur so frequently. A recent survey revealed that most working people's sons and daughters do not follow in their business, trade or profession. THE REASON: at home after work usually brings negative comments and problems about the job in front of the rest of the family. Thus, the impression is given to the offspring of a tedious and unfavorable job. Multiply this by weeks, months and years. Take this as a lesson and talk about the positive aspects of your hobby/business to your family.

ASK THEM THEIR OPINION(S) . . . Nothing recruits more allies than getting other's opinions and advice on what you are doing. Some people may know more than you do about your endeavor(s). When facing a decision, ask them their thoughts. You

may be surprised that they may think the same as you do, and this will fortify your decision.

ASK THEM FOR HELP . . . There are, no doubt, experts on something you are not such as financial, business, technical, marketing, etc. Search their brains; you'll be surprised what you will learn AND it will make them feel a part of your project, thus they will be more positive about the time and money you are spending on it!!!

SELL THEM A PARTNERSHIP OR INTEREST . . . Pay them back in a share of the profits according to their investment, like selling stock or part ownership.

NAME A PRODUCT AFTER THEM . . . If possible, what a great way to feed anyone's ego. This will get them on your side even more, especially if you are even mildly successful.

SHOW THEM YOU ARE SERIOUS . . . Put down the goals you are aspiring to obtain, share them. Set realistic deadlines. Set aside an area JUST for you and your creation such as the garage, attic, cellar, part of the family room or even the bedroom. Ask their help to build, move or create this area for you.

TOGETHER TIME . . . Do not use the time you normally spend with family to work on your creation. This will cause resentment.

SHARE YOUR ENTHUSIASM . . . By showing clear-cut goals, organization and enthusiasm, you will or should receive respect and encouragement. Let them realize that your hobby is an expression of you and your talents. Discuss the possibility of making money or recognition by marketing or presenting your work in a show. Together investigate the possibility of tax write-offs for house expenses.

SHARE THE REWARDS . . . The pride and accomplishments derived from creating and finishing should be shared with others in the family. Let them realize that your creation helps you feel relaxed and free from tension, depression and boredom. If they suggested something that worked, let them know it. Tell them you put their idea to work and it succeeded.

By applying some or all of these basic principles, your hobby (or if it is a business "cottage industry") will be more fun and more successful. The family can give you the reassurance and encouragement that we all thrive on and hunger for.

CHAPTER 9
LAWS, LICENSES, LIABILITIES & LEGALITIES

Lawyers, accountants, insurance agents, printers, wholesalers, salespeople all have to make money but let's not let them get rich from us!!!

A. LAWYERS

You won't use a lot of this information now but we are assuming that you will in the future **BECAUSE** you are going to be successful!!! REMEMBER you have to THINK SUCCESS TO BE SUCCESSFUL.

ATTORNEYS/LAWYERS/BARRISTERS/COUNSELORS . . . they all collect their fees from the public by selling their time and knowledge (and a lot of the time they have to ask others or look it up in those books that impress you as you enter his/her office.) Review these ideas before you make a decision:

1. What do I want to do — write a will, incorporate, sue someone, ask a legal question? Write it down on a piece of paper and ask yourself, ''Can I do it myself?'' ''Can I ask someone who is informed and who will not charge me $50-$150/hour for the answer?'' Many wills, incorporations, legal documents, real estate transactions, have documents that can be bought in an office supply store. They can be notarized and witnessed without spending a legal fee.

2. Ask a client about the attorney in question.

3. Can you go to a Legal Clinic (like a dental, medical clinic) for a more realistic fee?

4. If you need an attorney ask for a FREE consultation to make a decision.

5. Inspect the premises. If sloppy and outdated, chances are the attorney will be too.

6. Real plush with expensive furniture and decorations. Guess who paid for these . . . you bet, the clients.

7. Does the attorney take you on time or do you have to wait?

8. Does he/she have all interruptions and phone calls held while you are in the office?

9. Ask for a fee schedule. MOST people never do and this allows the lawyer a free hand when making out the bill.

10. Examine (slyly of course) how many "while-you-were-out" phone slips are on the desk. We went into one attorney's office and saw about 25 of these pink slips on his desk. This told us he either didn't have time or didn't want to return these calls. Some were 3-4 days old.

11. How organized is the desk and surrounding area(s)? Is it organized clutter or just a heap of junk? You can tell about his/her mental thinking by this observation.

12. Don't make a decision at this time. There is an overabundance of attorneys and when you are spending that kind of money take your time, unless you are out on bail and must have a trial lawyer immediately to fight that murder charge.

Choosing a lawyer is as important as choosing a physician. You should get the best for the least amount of money.

13. Sometimes it's cheaper to talk on the phone than spending so much time at the office.

14. You may change lawyers like you can any other service. You are not obligated to stay with the same one forever.

15. Check list for evaluating an attorney

    1. Do they keep me waiting long?

    2. Do they seem organized?

    3. Do they give me **undivided** attention (no phone calls, interruptions)?

4. How soon do they return my calls?

5. Can I get to them in an emergency?

6. Are the charges (fees) spelled out?

7. Are most decisions right?

8. What are their hourly fees?

9. Do I feel comfortable in his/her presence?

10. Do they have a good reputation?

B. INSURANCE AGENCIES

CHOOSING AN INSURANCE AGENT . . . another expense that we must live with.

Insurance agents are like car salesmen. They have outgoing personalities and earn their money by COMMISSION. That means the higher the price or the more they sell, the more they make. They are not trying to win a popularity contest. They want your money, not your friendship! When you are spending your hard-earned money, treat all business people the same.

Experts say that 1% of your business should be allocated to insurance expenditures. Most of us have very little knowledge of this business so we have to depend on an expert, or supposedly an expert. Does Allan sound bitter? Well, he is. He has run multi-million dollar corporations and small thousand-dollar home-based businesses. He has advised and been a paid consultant for other businesses. Out of all the insurance agents he has been in contact with, and that numbers in the dozens, he has yet to find one who is completely knowledgeable and dependable. What does this prove? It means that YOU have to know a few things BEFORE you let these people SELL you insurance.

Agents who sell life insurance work on a commission of 55% for the first year and 9% for the next five years. Casualty agents, the ones you and I need for fire and liability insurance, receive 10-15% of the premium you pay for as long as you pay.

CHECK LIST FOR CHOOSING
AN INSURANCE AGENT OR AGENCY

1. Draw up a list of your needs. Example: home, fire, liability comprehensive.

   a. Do you rent or lease? If you rent, your landlord has a blanket insurance policy on the structure and fixtures but NOT on the contents.

      1. You must have additional coverage for your furniture, TV, sewing machine, clothes, etc.

Determine how much these are worth. This will give you an idea of how much coverage you need.

2. Liability coverage (if someone falls, is injured, rips their clothing, etc.) Most often your home or apartment insurance policy will cover any possible problem with liabilities. You may have to have additional coverage for product liability (to cover any damage your product may do to a consumer, yes, even a cloth doll may cause allergy or irritation to some people). If you have a stock of expensive materials find out if you are covered. We have a collection of dolls. They are covered for theft, fire, etc., but not if they are broken.

Unfortunately there is always someone who wants to take advantage of a minor situation and SUE. We have to protect ourselves from these people.

3. Theft/burglary.

b. If you own, you already have insurance if you have a mortgage (the bank INSISTS on covering their property or investment). Most comprehensive homeowners policies have protection for theft and burglaries. You may have to buy additional coverage for equipment you use. Most sewing machines, computers, typewriters, etc. are covered. Find out!

c. PRODUCT LIABILITY. This is very inexpensive, it covers you in case the product hurts or damages something or someone.

2. Pick a company that is familiar with your kind of business. How do you find these companies? Ask someone who is already in the business.

3. Pick a well-established agency.

4. Pick a person whom you are compatible, someone who will spend time with you.

5. If a relative, realize you may have to turn them down or discharge them. Will this affect your relationship?

6. ALWAYS, ALWAYS have two quotes on your needs.

C. CHOOSING AN ACCOUNTANT

If you have a business, you will have to file with the IRS, EVEN if you do not make any money. For the few dollars extra we recommend that your yearly tax preparation by done by an accountant, preferably a CPA (Certified Public Accountant). Follow the same basic rules that we outlined in the attorney choosing article.

We have found in the years of doing business that the extra time and money spent on accountants was one of the best investments in business. They will show you how NOT to get in trouble with UNCLE (the IRS and state tax systems). It always pays to be honest, in fact it is much easier. You will have enough problems without having to look over your shoulder.

A few hints:

1. Find out their fees FIRST.

2. A larger firm will charge more. They have larger overhead (expenses).

3. Give them information in a readable, organized form.

4. Allow them enough time to prepare the information you need. Many of the offices put your info on a computer.

5. As with your attorney, BE HONEST. If you have done something wrong, take their advice, use it or ignore it.

6. I would strongly recommend avoiding the franchise, storefront firms. Some employ noncertified tax consultants.

D. SHOULD I "HIDE" OR "BURY" MY PROFITS?

Some people say "why all this fuss?" It seems that everyone is doing something on the side. These are called underground businesses. The IRS states that the amount of tax money uncollected equal that which is legally collected AND if all were collected it could wipe out the national debt in 5 years.

1. A business cannot prosper and thrive if it remains hidden. You have to deal with other "honest" businesses.

2. IF and WHEN you decide to sell a prosperous business how can you show the actual sales? Most buyers want a copy of the company's financial and income records. This verifies the sales volume.

3. You may become very successful and tax agencies want their share. They will ultimately become aware of you. If you have not conformed to the laws, then you can become liable for all previous unreported income. Once you have been investigated for unreported income, you can be sure of many more investigations.

4. A lot of people have a clear conscience. Any kind of illegal activity would make them suffer anxiety and stress.

5. Remember that that desk, chair, sewing machine, typewriter, calculator, etc. can be depreciated and used as a business expense, both of which are tax deductions.

6. You will want to register your business name or the name of your product to protect it.

E. LAWS AND LICENSES

Included are possible licenses you may need, even if it is a "home business." Some states have "Homework Laws." They may have some effect on your business. It seems that the states of California, Illinois, Pennsylvania, New Jersey and Puerto Rico prohibit toys and dolls from being made at home. These are old laws and unless you have a full-fledged factory I doubt if you will be bothered. It is best to check with your attorney.

NOTE: It is important to maintain a low profile (don't shake the neighbor's bush) because:

1. They may turn you in for operating a business.

2. The increased traffic may be annoying to them.

3. The IRS, local tax, and other agencies may start snooping.

4. If it looks good someone else will want to copy.

County Laws

1. Occupational licenses. Cities, towns or any other municipality may demand these licenses.

2. D/B/A (doing business as) or Fictitious Name Registration Affidavit. To have a legitimate business you have to register with the county. It requires a nominal fee and has to be advertised in a paid advertisement publication three consecutive times (may vary).

State Laws

1. A state tax number for state sales tax (if applicable).

2. Corporation reports and taxes, usually to the Secretary of State at the state capitol.

Federal Laws

1. IRS. Don't have to say too much about this agency.

2. If you employ others, then all kinds of laws and taxes apply.

3. Small Business Administration (SBA) — agency to apply to for loans.

Regional

1. Better Business Bureau. If you plan on a long-range business it's always beneficial to register with this agency. Many established businesses will agree that BBB does little good for you. It is not possible to use their name in advertising or as a reference. The only time you come in contact with them is if you are doing something wrong, or have upset a customer.

2. Consumer Protection agencies. They may be called by a different name but most counties, cities or states have one. These protect the consumer from fly-by-night and illegal businesses.

F. COPYRIGHT LAWS

There are some people who start a business and infringe upon the intellectual property of others, property which is protected by the Copyright Law. Most people do not understand this law and often break it. As a businessperson you must be knowledgeable of this federal law.

To find out more about this law and to quote an expert we called the Federal Information Number (which should be in the front of your phone book) and asked who to call for this information. We talked to Chris Collious of the Copyright Office in Washington.

The copyright law was enacted in 1790 and most recently amended in January, 1978. It is designed to protect the rights of creators of intellectual property in seven broad categories of work:

1. literary works

2. musical works, and accompanying words

3. dramatic works, and accompanying music

4. pantomimes and choreographic works

5. pictorial, graphic, and sculptural works

6. motion pictures and other audiovisual works

7. sound recordings

To avoid violating the copyright law, you must learn to recognize and respect all work that is protected by it. A properly copyrighted work of any kind will bear a notice containing these three essential elements:

1. the word "copyright" or its abbreviation, "copr.", or the copyright symbol, ©

2. the year of first publication of the work (when it was first shown or sold to the public)

3. the name of the copyright owner. Sometimes the words, "All Rights Reserved" will also appear, which means that copyright protection has been extended to include all of the Western Hemisphere.

Copyright protection for works created after January 1, 1978 lasts for the life of the author or creator plus fifty years after death. If you make a one-of-a-kind item and there are designs or images you wish to protect, be sure to include the proper copyright notice on each item you offer for sale. Your copyright can be conveyed to others only in writing. You may be able to make a Muppet with the approval of the owner and the payment of certain royalties. There are some who have copied E.T., Annie, Raggedy Ann, the Campbell Kids. They are doing this illegally and may open themselves up to litigation.

It does not cost anything to place the copyright symbol and wording on any item, BUT you cannot sue or prevent others from using it without paying the $10 fee and registering with the United States Copyright Office, Library of Congress, Washington, D.C. 20559.

1. Form SE for a serial, periodicals, newspapers, magazines, bulletins, newsletters, annuals, journals, and proceedings of societies.

2. Form TX for nondramatic literary works, including books, directories and other works written in words. This includes How-To instructions for a craft project.

3. Form VA for visual arts, such as graphic, pictorial or sculptural works.

4. Form PA for the performing arts.

5. Form SR for sound recordings.

Send $10 and two copies of the "best edition" of the work.

WHAT CANNOT BE COPYRIGHTED
1. Names, titles, and short phrases (see Trade mark)

2. Inventions (see patents)

3. Ideas

NOTE: The artwork of the Cabbage Patch Kid can be copyrighted. The name can be trademarked and the ingredients or materials can be patented.

G. PATENTS
The U.S. government issues a grant giving an inventor the right to excude others from making, using or selling the invention

within the U.S. It lasts for 17 years and an attorney may cost you from $3,000-$10,000. For information ask for the book "General Information Concerning Patents" from Superintendent of Documents, Washington, D.C. 20559.

H. TRADEMARK

This includes any word, name, symbol or device or any combination used by a manufacturer or merchant to identify his goods. Its function is to indicate origin and it serves as a guarantee of quality. You must use your trademark to establish it. It must be used at least once in interstate commerce (between states). Patent and Trademark Office, Superintendent of Documents, Washington, D.C. 20559.

I. IS IT A BUSINESS OR HOBBY?

IRS WOULD LIKE TO KNOW

If you are deducting expenses the IRS has a few guidelines for you to follow. The distinction between a hobby and a business is a very fine line. You must be able to prove that you intend to make a profit.

WHAT THE IRS WILL LOOK AT TO MAKE THE DISTINCTION

Things to remember:

1. You must show profit two of the five years to use deductible expenses. How many of us could last that long without making a profit?

2. You can delay any IRS determination until the first five years are used up by filing a special form.

3. Keep accurate books and records to prove you operate in a businesslike manner.

4. You institute new operating procedures to correct losses.

5. You operate in a professional way. You have an attorney, an accountant, etc.

6. You have made a serious effort to establish the business.

7. There is a profit potential.

8. You have had past successes.

9. You have registered your name with the county clerk.

10. You have business cards and/or stationery.

11. You have a listing in the Yellow Pages.

12. You keep a log of business.

13. You have advertised in local papers.

14. You have a business bank account.

15. You have bought a postage meter.

16. You have a business phone.

17. Is it just a pleasurable venture, for instance horseracing or antiques? (Car racing people have a tough time proving their intent.)

CHAPTER 10
BUYING YOUR MATERIALS

Logically when you first start out, you will have to buy materials at the local fabric or department store. Many stores have remnants and closeouts that you could take advantage of. Go to the library and search out some catalog books: **The Wholesale by Mail Catalog** — 175 5th Ave., N.Y., N.Y. 10010 and **The Great Book of Catalogs** — 135 Oak Terrace, Lake Bluff, Ill. 60044.

Another thought — buy ready made clothing that has been put on sale because of outdating or damage. You can get some expensive materials for very little money. A lot of dolls' dresses can be made from a woman's skirt, dress or a man's dress shirt.

Remember, never try to cheat the customer. Always use new material unless you are producing a craft item. Then, anything goes in order to get the right effect. Make sure all old and used items are clean and fresh.

Don't forget to save the buttons, zipper and trim. They all can be made use of.

If you are going to register your business and get a tax number

from the state tax agency, then you can present this number any time you buy materials and not have to pay tax. Conversely, when you sell your product, you will have to charge tax and fill out the tax forms and send them to the state every month.

After you get your volume up, you will be able to wheel and deal. You can buy bolts of materials or dozens of items. Then you can dicker with the manager or owner for a better price. Your next step would be to order direct and that is an education by itself!

KEEP TRACK of your material expenditures. It will help you determine whether or not you are making money.

WAYS TO SAVE MONEY AND BUY WHOLESALE

A successful business person has to buy low and sell high to pay expenses and make a profit. Here are some suggestions that we have gathered from years in business:

1. Create an identity. You must be an authentic "business" for the wholesalers to take you seriously.

    a.   Have a business or product name.

    b.   Register your name with the proper agency (usually the County).

    c.   Obtain a tax number with the State. This is one of the most obvious ways to be legitimate.

    d.   Have calling cards, stationery etc.

    e.   Be listed in the Yellow Pages

2. When starting out, combine your needs and ask the independent supplier for a "professional" discount, usually 20%.

3. Use your tax number to save paying tax. You must then charge tax when you sell your completed product.

4. Find mail order wholesalers who will sell to you direct. Ask questions, look on packages and copy addresses. We have found many sources this way.

5. Be PATIENT and PERSISTENT. Always use your business stationery and type, not hand write, your communications.

6. Send your first order in with the full payment. Take 2% cash discount if allowed.

7. For Toy, Hobbies, Craft supplies — **Playthings Directory** ($3), 51 Madison Ave., N.Y., N.Y. 10010.

8. A great book that will show you how to sell to catalog houses. **SELLING TO CATALOG HOUSES** ($15), Box 10423,

Springfield, MO 65808.

9. **WHERE TO SELL IT DIRECTORY** ($3.50), 103 Cooper St., Babylon, N.Y. 11702.

10. The trade magazine for those involved in the garment industry. **WOMENS WEAR DAILY**, 7 E. 12th, N.Y., N.Y. 10003.

11. Call your phone business office and get copies of the Yellow Pages from the big cities — New York, Los Angeles and Chicago. You will find unlimited sources of wholesale buying.

12. Get **CATALOG SOURCES FOR CREATIVE PEOPLE**, H.P. Books, 5367 (Box), Tucson, AZ 85703.

13. Obtain the book on 800 telephone numbers (library or book store). It can save you a lot in long distance calls.

14. The **AMERICAN MANUFACTURERS, THOMAS REGISTER** at your library will list ALL of the manufacturers of supplies.

15. Send all orders in on a purchase order form with a purchase order number on it (at your stationery store) to save time and expense.

16. If you belong to an organization, club or association, pool your needs and buy together for quantity discounts. If you don't have a club, think of forming one.

17. Watch the papers, (yours and those in cities near you) for closeouts and going-out-of-business sales.

18. **APPAREL INDUSTRY MAGAZINE**, 6226 Vineland Ave., N. Hollywood, CA 91006. This is a national directory of suppliers and contractors in the apparel industry. ALWAYS ASK FOR FREE COPIES OF THESE MAGAZINES AND CATALOGS.

19. AMERICAN HOME SEWING ASSOCIATION publishes a directory of the shows they put on with names, addresses and dates. 1270 Broadway, N.Y., N.Y. 10001.

20. NATIONAL NEEDLEWORK ASSOCIATION INC. publishes **National Needlework News** and sponsor a major needlework trade market TNNA show. 230 5th Ave., N.Y. N.Y. 10001.

21. **CREATIVE PRODUCTS.** FREE subscription if you are in the business and have AUTHENTICITY! Box 584, Lake Forest, IL 60045.

22. **CREATIVE MONEY & HOMEMADE MONEY**. Barbara Brabec. A great guide for those in the home-based business. For info Box 10632 Riviera Beach, FL 33404, Success Publications.

23. **SEW BUSINESS**, Box 1331, Ft. Lee, N.J. 07024. For retailers in home-sewing, quilting and needlework merchandise.

24. **SEW NEWS**. The newspaper for people who sew. 208 S. Main, Seattle, WA 98104. A must for those in the sewing business. LOADED with money saving ideas. A bimonthly newspaper.

These are just a few suggestons that may help you when you decide to market your product. It takes a lot of research, question asking and reading. "The person who digs the deepest finds the most gold."

The library is a great source for directories that can give tons of information for buying sewing materials.

1. The **Standard Periodical Directory** contains descriptive listings for more than 60,000 consumer magazines, trade journals, directories, etc. You will find sources that you may never come in contact with, magazines that never are placed on the reading racks you see. There are organizations that may help you, newsletters that will give you ideas.

Note: Write on your advertising company stationery and ask for R&D (rate and data) info and a "REVIEW" copy, not a sample copy. You MAY want to advertise your product after you have found out about their rates.

2. **Ayer Directory of Newspapers and Periodicals**
3. ULRICH'S **International Periodicals Directory**
4. **Books in Print**
5. **Guide to Forthcoming Books**
6. **Consumer Magazine** and **Agri-Media Rates and Data**
7. **Literary Market Place**
8. **Encyclopedia of Associations**
9. **Directory of Directories**
10. **Thomas Register of American Manufacturers**

All these library sources will give you numerous possibilities of material sources, books to help you in every aspect of producing, marketing, selling and managing your business.

In a 1984 edition of **WOMAN'S WORLD** there was an article about Margaret Boyd. She has compiled a 208-page **SEW AND SAVE SOURCE BOOK** (Success Publications, Box 10632, Riviera Beach, FL, 33404) ($9.95). It contains sources for equipment, notions, fabrics, leather, trims, infant's and children's wear, bridal accessories, dolly and toy making supplies, etc. Many of the supplies are available at wholesale and discount prices.

CHAPTER 11
HOW TO GET PEOPLE TO BUY
MY CREATION(S)

Up to this point we have done a lot of preparation. We have made the decision to go into a business. We have named the product, have established a plan. We have looked at the competition and decided whether we will do it at home or rent a store. Our finances are in order; we have a budget and a plan. We have examined the local laws and licensing. Attorneys, accountants, insurance agencies have been obtained. We have found a way to get the rest of our family and friends as excited about our venture as we are. We now have to explore the areas of SELLING the product to someone who has COLD CASH in their hands.

It is very important that we have done the above to be able to SELL EFFECTIVELY. Many go into business without this basic thinking and planning. Their chances of succeeding are very slim. YOU will be able to make better decisions and bring more money into the TILL.

NOTE: WE SUGGEST THOSE WHO WANT A SHORTCUT TO IGNORE THE PREVIOUS CHAPTERS AND START HERE!

A. A CHECK LIST

1. I have made the commitment to go ahead, not to go halfway into the stream and turn around and go back.
____YES ____NO

2. I have the ability (time, enthusiasm, desire) to go ahead.
____YES____NO

3. I have the talent to produce a saleable product.
____YES____NO

4. I have tested my product on friends and relatives to see if it is acceptable.
____YES____NO

5. I have established an identity (business name, applied for a license, procured business supplies).
____YES____NO

6. I am prepared to put that EXTRA effort into making MY business a SUCCESS!
____YES____NO

7. I fully realize that there may be some hurdles and problems as I grow.
____YES____NO

8. I have named the product and/or the business and have made calling cards, statonery, etc.
____YES____NO

9. I have physically established a plan.
____YES____NO

10. I have closely examined any competition and KNOW MINE IS BETTER!
____YES____NO

11. I have established a budget and realize the cost to produce my product.
____YES____NO

12. I have obtained or can obtain financing.
____YES____NO

13. I have made the decision of operating from my home or from a rented store.
____YES____NO

14. I have enthusiastically tried to win over my family so that I will have support and encouragement.
____YES____NO

15. I have obtained information on who or IF I need profes-

56

sional help (attorney, accountant, insurance etc.).
____YES____

16. I have examined local zoning laws.
____YES____NO

17. I have obtained necessary business licenses.
____YES____NO

18. I have made tax-reporting requirements.
____YES____NO

19. I am satisfied that the IRS will be satisfied with the structure of my business venture.
____YES____NO

20. I have looked into copyrights, patents, etc.
____YES____NO

21. I have gathered sources to buy materials at the lowest price.
____YES____NO

22. I have examined the possibility of obtaining a copyright, patent, or trademark.

B. TESTING THE PRODUCT FIRST

1. Make one or two to start.

2. Ask your friends, family, enemies, store owners, anyone, who will give you an honest evaluation.

3. LISTEN to their opinions.

4. Make an inexpensive slinger/brochure first.

5. Do not invest in any major equipment in the beginning.

6. ADVERTISING: place classified ads in your local paper with different wording and keep track of responses.

7. Find a 500-1000 names and address list and TEST with your mailing piece (slinger). It is recommended that you have to have at least 1000 to get an honest testing. If you get ½ to 2% responses with money, consider it GOOD, any more and you've got a WINNER.

8. Carefully figure how much it will cost you to put the product in the consumers' hands. Remember our lesson in the BUDGET chapter that the cost is more than the material, thread and packaging.

9. Determine if you can produce enough of the product to make enough money for your efforts.

10. Determine if you can produce a LARGE amount if asked to.

11. EXAMINE possible sources of advertising — magazines, annuals, newsletters and newspapers. (A good source for all these is *THE WRITERS MARKER,* 9933 Alliance Rd., Cincinnati, OH 45242 or at your book store). Send postcards and ask for their RATE & DATA SHEETS. These are their advertising charges and usually the publishers will send you a review copy.

12. Determine how much money you have to spend.

13. See if you can CONSIGN your product in a retail store. Read the chapter on CONSIGNMENT and make a decision if it is a good move for YOU.

14. BEFORE you start investigate sources for your materials, see if you can buy at the least possible cost.

15. Make sure that your product can be packaged and shipped easily and economically. If you are making bedspreads, the shipping cost may double the selling price because of the bulk and weight.

C. MARKETING IDEAS

There have been thousands of books written and millions of dollars spent trying to figure the correct method to get the public to buy products.

YOUR CHECKLIST BEFORE DETERMINING YOUR MARKETING AREA(S)

1. Make out a budget.

2. Determine how many you want to (or can) produce. What if you get a company that calls one day and orders 575 blouses or soft dolls? WE have heard of this happening.

3. Determine how much the product costs. (Include all materials, overhead, and labor.)

4. How much do you have to spend on marketing?

5. Can I expand if need be?

6. Who can I help if I have to produce quantity?

7. Make out a **Marketing Plan:**

	Date Completed	**By**
Product definition		
Product material cost		

Product overhead cost . . . .
Number hours and minutes to produce .
Total amount of product cost . . . .
Design of package . . . .
Printing work . . . .
Packaging . . . .
Mailing/shipping/delivery costs . . . .
Advertising/marketing budget . . . .
Tracking charts made and used . . . .

D. ADVERTISING

Unfortunately your enthusiasm for your new product is not known to the general public. Somehow they, the public, must be informed of your business and product. This is called advertising. Listed are some of ithe less expensive ways to start off:

1. **Brochure . . .** This can be hand made, hand typed, hand lettered and copied as follows:

     a.   The most expensive — a printer
     b.   Copied at a copying store, about $12.00/500
     c.   Mimeographed at a school or church
     d.   Copied at a friend's or relative's photo copy machine, offer to pay exact cost for paper, etc.

Make sure the artwork is professionally done by an artist friend. A drawing or photo ALWAYS attracts the reader much more often than just plain printing.

DISTRIBUTION

1.   Hand deliver them to area homes.
2.   Pay paperboy to include in newspaper (might not be legal, but worth trying).
3.   Ask area merchants if you can leave them on their counters. Many will be glad to help you.
4.   Put one on ALL area bulletin boards. (Usually found in supermarkets, drugstores, restaurants, bars, etc.)
5.   Deliver one to every business in your area . . . office buildings, plazas, malls, REMEMBER, the more original and enthusiastic you are, the more possibility of success.
6.   Some Pennysavers/Shopping Guides will include them for very little money — 3/4 to 1-1/2 cents each.
7.   Area newspapers will include them on a specific day and a specific area of your choosing.

2. **Want Ad/Classified ads:** You should ALWAYS TEST an idea first when advertising. The best way is to put an inexpensive ad in the want ads. It will cost you from $1.00 to $5.00 depending on the circulation of the paper. (They charge you more if they distribute more papers, less if they distribute less.) Do not place a display ad (a single 1'' up column ad) until you are fairly successful. The want-ad will show you how interested the public is with your endeavor. If you receive a few responses the first time, change the wording and place it in again. If you receive a lot DO NOT change the wording and repeat the ad. Rule of thumb, ''If you are successful with a particular advertising method, repeat it until it wears out.'' The best place to start is your local Pennysaver or Shopping Guide. They are the least expensive (because they are limited in circulation and area covered) and will get your message to YOUR area, not an area twenty miles away. When, and if, you become more successful and want to expand, then you can place an ad in your morning or evening paper. Some small towns and cities combine a type of Pennysaver/Shoppers Guide newspaper together. It always is smart to ask for and compare advertising rates and PAID circulation. Some publications PRINT a lot but sell very few. You see these in free paper boxes and on store shelves, waiting for someone to pick them up.

3. **WORD OF MOUTH . . .** Probably the most powerful and lasting of all the advertising!! Your reputation, dependability, quality of work, product offered, price and many more aspects of you and your business can be and will be spread by people who have been satisfied or dissatisfied. Even one dissatisfied person can damage your business. Every person has at least 200 people they can influence in their work, home or social contracts. So, reputation is one of the more lasting ways of advertising your business.

4.**RADIO/TV . . .** We don't think these areas of advertising are what you are ready for at this time. Very expensive and very spotty.

5. **DISPLAY ADVERTISING . . .** After you have established yourself and are on your way to a successful career, you may want to expand or enlarge your volume of business. This kind of ad is a ''free standing ad'' in any one of the before mentioned papers. They are sometimes noticed more easily than the want ad BUT many times a small ad will get buried among larger ones or put on the bottom inside area of the paper. You don't have a choice of the position when placing a display ad in most papers. You take your position by chance. It is always thought that the frequent advertisers receive the better position. You should spend a lot of time on constructing this ad, as it is expensive and is competing with a lot of professionals. Don't let this faze you. Some

of the most successful businesses have lousy unappealing advertising. It is your objective to stop the readers' eyes at your ad. Thousands of books have been written on this subject, still it is a chance. Don't fill the ad with too much copy. Glance through papers and determine what stops your eyes. Is it a picture, is it contrasting colors (or black and white) or a word? Ask friends and family their opinion. The only right answer is when you receive calls or orders from the ad. Again, test it small before going hog wild.

6. **FREEBIES, COUPONS, TWO FOR ONE** . . . These are all gimmicks to get people to buy a service or product. It has been used for years and is very successful. You have probably taken advantage of these many times. McDonald's give coupons for free cokes, etc. You see coupons in the paper all the time offering cents off if you buy their product. Some businesses have penny sales (buy the first one, get the second for a penny). Buy one type of product and get another free. Buy one year subscription to a magazine and get another book free. What about "Book and Record of the Month Clubs" . . . ten for 1 cent . . . they get you in as a member and obligate you to buy so many in so much time. Maybe you could offer one extra month's service free if the customer signs up and pays in advance for one year. If offering a low cost product you may offer one free when buying twelve (very commonly used in the drug/grocer retail business). Remember, you want to give better service, more quality or more goods for the same price OR LOWER than any competitor.

7. **SIGNAGE** . . . Vehicle, it doesn't matter whether you use a wagon, skate board, bike, moped, cycle, car, truck, van, bus semi, train, plane, hot air balloon, submarine or by foot, you should carry or have a sign advertising your business. How many people do you think you pass every day? Could be in the thousands, and with an imprinted T-shirt, bumper sticker or sign it can mean extra business.

8. **CALLING CARDS, STATIONERY** . . . In all the years and business we have been in, or advised, very few have warranted the expenditure of monies on these items, especially at first. The only thing it will do is to boost your ego. I would advise an inexpensive calling card **OR** a different approach, for instance, your message on a wooden nickel, a round tuit plastic coin or something that will make you remembered. Don't go crazy and order stationery, bill heads, receipts, etc. You can buy standard job order forms, bill heads, receipts at your local office supply store for a fraction of what it would cost to have imprinted. (The cheapest calling card price I have seen . . . pick up a copy of *The Wall Street Journal* . . . Stationery House offers 500 calling cards for $7.50).

61

9. **FREE RADIO/TV ADVERTISING . . .** Many times stations have room for unique human interest stories. If you think you have something different to tell, contact your local radio or TV station and take your chances. But you also run the risk of letting someone else know of your success and decide to get in the same business. This would dilute or diminish the potential market or business potential for you. Only you can decide on this.

E. FORMING AN ADVERTISING COMPANY

It is a known fact that the media gives a RECOGNIZED advertising company 15% discount and a 2% discount if paid with 10 to 30 days. If you plan to advertise, buy mailing lists and products, the time and money spent to form a company is well worth the effort. Here are the steps involved:

1. Think up a name.

2. Open a bank account. This may be difficult unless you have a good relationship with your banker. You will have to present a profit and loss and balance sheet OR show them the "fictitious name certificate."

3. Obtain a fictitious name certificate of a D/B/A (doing business as) at the county you live in. You will pay a nominal fee and have the name printed in three editions of a paid circulation newspaper. This is the same procedure that you went through to register your business.

4. Apply for a tax number at the state building. This is optional.

5. Have stationery AND standard advertising order forms printed (see example).

6. USE IT . . . every time you advertise, even a classified ad, send it out on your official stationery. (Classified ads DO NOT allow the 15% discount). Use it to communicate.

7. Ask your business friends if you can send their ads in on your order blanks and stationery. We have used ours for the NDSA Doll organization, Dollsense Newsletter, Academy of Continuing Educational Seminars, Allan Smith Seminars and the books we have published. Over the years we have gained creditability and CREDIT from many media such as *Wall Street Journal, Writers Digest,* etc.

8. Do not misuse this privilege.

9. You wil have to send advertising material camera ready.

10. Use it to obtain advertising prices (called R and D information, rate and data) from publications where you may want to advertise.

11. Ask for a review copy. There are thousands of magazines published but very few are available on the magazine racks.

12. If you have a business phone, make your advertising business listed in the Yellow Pages.

13. TRACKING CHARTS (Example A) . . . If you advertise in any manner you should have TRACKING CHARTS evaluate the results. Example:

SUCCESS ADVERTISING TRACKING CHART (MASTER) (a)

ORDER NUMBER	CODE	DATE PLACED	MEDIA	ISSUE & RELEASE DATE	COST	BOOK
D 301	SMITH	5-23-84	DOWLING SCIENCE	AUG- 7/17	123.60	101
D 302	SUCCESS	5-23-84	MECHANIX ILLUST	SEP- 8/6	101.20	101
D 303	ALLAN SMITH	6-17-84	WRITERS DIGEST	SEPT- 8/30	97.75	WS
D 304	SUCCESS BOOK	6-15-84	WALL STREET JOURNAL	7-13-84	516.17	WS
D 305	ALLAN	6-30-84	FAMILY CIRCLE	OCT 2	304.66	SFP
D 306	SFP	6-29-84	WOMANS CIRCLE	SEPT	249.90	SFP
D 307	SMPUB	7-10-84	BETTER HOMES & GARDEN	NOV/DEC- SEPT	1141.00	SFP
D 308	ENMPUB	7-10-84	McCALLS	NOV/OCT- SEPT	512.00	SFP
D 309	SEWING	7-17-84	SEW NEWS	NOV- OCT-11th	212.41	SFP
D 310	SMITH	7-17-84	WORK BASKET	OCT SEPT 5th	63.70	SFP

a. This is a master chart that will show the complete advertising picture. The ORDER NUMBER is placed on the ORDER SHEET (b) CODING: this is to help determine from which ad you got your response. In this way you can learn which ad is drawing the best. As you can see, we have listed the response name as SMITH one time and SUCCESS another time. Ways to code your ad.

1. Change the spelling of your name — Smith, Smythe, Scmith.
2. Change the spelling of your street . . . Main, Maine, Mainne, Mayne.
3. Use a department number — D 301, Dept. MS, etc. I don't like this because most people know it is a code and are naturally lazy and will not write more than they have to.
4. Use a completely different name.

It is important that you don't change it too radically, only enough so the post person will still delivery it.

(Example b.) ORDER SHEET . . . This is an easy professional way to submit ads. Always keep a copy and record it on the TRACKING CHART.

(Example c.) RESPONSE CHART . . . Every time you get an answer, the date and the amount of responses you receive should be recorded. This will show you when you can expect results from your ad.

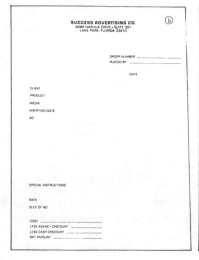

64

(Example d.) PUBLICITY TRACKING CHART . . . When you send publicity releases to various media you can record your follow-ups and so forth.

F. GETTING FREE OR LOW COST PUBLICITY

1. LOCAL NEWSPAPERS . . . The name NEWS is just what it means. Newspapers are starving for local news about local people. THE SECRET:

    a.   Send a formal press release (there is a certain style that most editors like to have (see example e).

    b.   Call the city desk of your newspaper and tell them about your HOMEMADE product. Inform them why, how, and when you started. Make an interesting human interest story and they will pay attention. We have advised people of this and have seen two-page spreads written about them. One article was about a stained glass artist, another was a gal who made ethnic soft dolls. The dolls were black, oriental and hispanic. Not colored white dolls but with the facial characteristics of the particular race.

2. LOCAL RADIO SHOWS . . . Most radio stations have talk shows. Some are at night, some at prime time. They are always looking for human interest stories. May I REPEAT! Don't make your story commercial, give it a personal touch and the commercialization will seep out naturally.

3. LOCAL TV STATIONS . . . The same as radio, a local morning show or evening show may want to interview you.

4. LOCAL PENNYSAVERS AND SHOPPERS GUIDES . . . They would love that story to fill in the paper.

5. LOCAL MERCHANTS . . . You can have low-cost slingers made up and photocopied. Ask the small independent merchants if you may leave a stack on their counters.

6. BULLETIN BOARDS . . . Have a small card or ad that you can tack on every B.B. with which you come in contact.

7. PERSONAL DELIVERY . . . Have your kids, friends or dogs put your sales message on the windshields of cars in parking lots.

8. CONSIGNMENT . . . Ask a local sewing store or craft store if you can put one of your products in stock. They only pay if they sell it.

9. EXCHANGE . . . IF you have a shop, put your display in their store in exchange for their display in yours.

10. IN PRINT . . . Have a brochure or slinger made up that will explain your product. Leave one on every counter or desk you pass. This has to generate some interest even if it is GET THIS D--- THING OFF MY COUNTER.

11. TALK about your product (without being obnoxious). Ask any advertiser and they will admit the best and cheapest advertisement is WORD OF MOUTH!

12. VOLUNTEER to give talks to local organizations and schools on how to make this particular product. The public is always interested in "How To" items.

13. TEACH a class at the local college, university, trade or high school adult education courses. June Ackerman of Atlanta, Georgia started with one sewing class and now has schools begging her to repeat the program at their locations. Her classes are always overfilled. Recently she is putting together a workbook to sell.

14. WRITE an article, send it to a sewing magazine such as *Sew News, Sewing, Better Homes & Garden Needlework and Crafts, McCalls Needlework and Crafts.* (See chapter on Teaching, Writing and Lecturing).

G. USING THE TELEPHONE

For you who are operating out of your homes, let's share some facts about the home phone. We have gone through this growing stage.

1. If you are alone, you MUST have an answering service OR an answering machine. You could miss that important call that could cost a lot of dollars.

2. The phone should be answered professionally. We have five children. Sometimes the caller is greeted with a grunt or "who is it?" to one of the dogs panting in the mouthpiece.

3. Many messages never get recorded correctly or are forgotten or transcribed incorrectly.

4. If you are selling nationally, the other time zones may want to call you at 5:00 a.m. or 11:00 at night. Are you prepared for this?

5. Can you keep your business phone expenses separately for tax purposes?

6. Will a phone call for business upset or interrupt the other family members? After years of hassle, missed and incorrect messages, Judy and I have just had another line installed in the house. This will be used for all of the business calls we both have. When we are not available we have an answering service. The cost is about $50/month for the line and the service. The service will answser "Thanks for calling 626-4643." Between the two of us we have about six different HOME-BASED businesses. (Don't tell our neighbors.)

I would suggest using your phone number in all your promotions and advertising. It can add 20 to 30% in business ESPECIALLY if you have MASTER/VISA. When you really get rolling get an 800 number. You can rent a number. You pay so much for another company to take your calls. (They could be 2000 miles away.) For a fee they can take messages, and many other kinds of valuable service. This costs about $60-100/month plus.
NOTE: Try to NOT sell without prepayment or a charge card. Your billings, follow-ups and deadbeats will cause you all kinds of work. GET THE MONEY UP FRONT!

H. PROMOTIONAL ITEMS

Get some postage-affixed postcards (used to be called penny postcards) and write for catalogs. The products may be able to help you make money.

TROPHIES, awards, prize ribbons — Dinn Bros., 68 Winter St., Box 111, Holyoke, MA 01041.

SPORTSWEAR ... imprinted hats, scarves, sweaters, t-shirts, sweatshirts — C&P Distributors, 32-02 Queens Blvd., Long Island City, N.Y. 11101.

BADGES, balloons frisbees, decals, hats imprinted with message — Special Events, Box 8, St. Charles, Minn. 55972.

BUMPER STICKERS, decals — Northwood Screen Printing, 1137 53rd Ct., Mangonia Park, FL 33407.

T-SHIRTS, jackets . . . imprinted — Primo Enterprises, 36-25 35th St., Long Island City, N.Y. 11106.

BOXES — U.S. Box, 1298 McCarter Hwy., Newark, N.J. 07504.

LABELS, stickers (mini) — Bucher Bros., 729 Leo St., Dayton, Ohio 45404.

PLASTIC BOXES — Creative Packaging, 770 Garrison Ave., Bronx, N.Y. 10474-5693.

BUSINESS CARDS . . . Great price . . . Ad always in *Wall Street Journal* — Stationery House, 1000 Florida Ave., Hagerstown, MD 21741.

CHARTS, appointment books — Caddylak Systems, 201 Montrose Rd., Westbury, N.Y. 11590.

BINDERS, folders — 20th Century Plastics, 3628 Crebshaw Blvd., Box 3763, L.A., CA 90051.

NOTEBOOKS, folders — American Thermoplastic Co., 622 Second Ave., Pittsburgh, PA 15219.

NOTEBOOKS, folders — Vulcan, Box 29, Vincent, AL 35178.

DISPLAY products — Siegel Display, Box 95, Minn., MN 55440.

SOURCE BOOKS, graphs, charts, forms that you can copy on a copier — Caddylak Systems, 201 Montrose Rd., Westbury, N.Y. 11590.

FILING systems — Jeffco, 205 Hallock, Box V, Middlesex, N.Y. 08846.

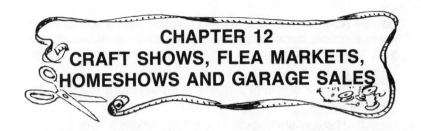

CHAPTER 12
CRAFT SHOWS, FLEA MARKETS,
HOMESHOWS AND GARAGE SALES

Here is a great way to get attention and sales for your product or creation. The originator of the Cabbage Patch Kids peddled his creations from fair to fair for years before they became a national sensation. The Hula Hoop was started the same way at local county fairs. Here are some suggestions and facts that may help you make a decision about renting that table, booth or space:

1. Realize that you must have an eye-appealing display. You have to get the attendee to STOP at your place to look and to BUY.

2. Have enough stock to satisfy the demands to buy your creation.

3. Be attentive when you are there. A turnoff to the public is to have a bored disinterested person at the table or booth reading a book.

4. Bring refreshments and things to keep you busy. You may sit for hours without talking or seeing anyone. Then again you may be so busy you won't have time for that cup of coffee. If you are alone, find someone who can relieve you when you go to the washroom. Drink very few liquids. Presidents, kings and

queens have to limit their intake of liquids before appearing at some function. Because of security reasons a queen can't just say, "Would anyone like to join me? I have to go to the Ladies Room."

5. Have a brochure/slinger and calling cards to give to interested people.

6. Have a note book to record suggestions people make or that you notice. Also for follow-up sales calls.

7. If possible have a Master/Visa card account. Your local banker can advise you on this. **This can increase sales up to 30%.**

8. Always get at least a 50% deposit on special orders that people request.

9. If it is cold have enough clothing. If in the sun and heat have shade and appropriate clothing.

10. Keep your eyes open. Unfortunately there are some who may want to steal your goods. Keep your money out of sight. If it gets to be a large amount have it secured or taken away.

11. Be patient and friendly to all. Be prepared to answer all kinds of questions from "where did you buy the material" to "where is the Men's Room?"

12. Wear a uniform or shirt that advertises your creation. There are many t-shirt stores that can make up one for you. You are a sewing professional; you should make an apron, hat etc. to make **you** stand out.

13. Have a price list and stick to it UNLESS you are prepared to haggle over prices. In some countries in the world this is the custom, to play the price game.

14. If you want to participate in a large county or state fair, you must make plans about six months ahead of time. You must reserve a space, send in a deposit and make plans.

15. Start with a small craft show first, analyze your successes, then make the decision whether or not to move to a larger affair.

16. Make an effort to find out how many people are expected (from past shows' attendance) and have enough handouts, etc.

17. If you are doing the show with friends or family set up a work schedule, write it out beforehand and make it CLEAR to everyone involved.

18. Find out what is furnished. Do they have tables and chairs, etc? Here is a check list that may help you:

Date of show	Parking
Place of show	Security during show
Times open	Security when closed
What is provided	Lighting
Electrical outlets	Heat/cooling
Restrooms	Water
Set-up times	Refreshments
Close-up/packing time	Pre and post set-up times
Approximate attendance	Deposit
Size of booth/display area	Cancellation fees
Cost of booth/display area	Wrapping materials (bags etc.)
Person in charge	Change (silver/dollars)
Sales slips	Tax records
Local ordinances	

19. Is what you are selling enough to cover your show expenses?

20. Does your price list reflect quantity discounts and wholesale prices?

21. Take a beginning inventory and an ending inventory. Compare it with the sales slips. This way you can determine what was stolen or not recorded.

22. Research the price you put on your creations. Is it too high or too low? Compare with similar items that other sell.

23. Determine if you are going to let the public "dicker" with prices. We recommend not doing this. You have worked hard to make your creation; stick to the original price. If you want to "close-out" an item THEN discount it.

24. Make sure EVERYTHING is marked and preferably with labels or stickers that cannot be removed or switched.

25. Have a procedure for customer or special orders. Either get full price up front or a 50% deposit.

26. Have a sign-in book AND get the addresses of all your customers. You can use these for direct mail sales. We have seen some sharp exhibitors run a FREE DRAWING. They collect hundreds of addresses that way. You can give away one of your creations and use the addresses to send sales information later.

27. An idea for a change box is to use a fishing tackle box. (Make sure you take enough change.)

28. Decide if you will accept personal checks or not. We suggest you accept them.

29. See if you can arrange with your bank to take Master/Visa.

30. You will be asked to give senior citizens discounts. Make that decision and put it on your price list.

31. Check out sources for bags and wrapping materials.

32. If a demonstration will help sell your product GO FOR IT! Did you ever see the way glass blowers or pottery makers stop traffic? You could take along your sewing machine. This would keep you busy during slack times, help to produce more products and be a show stopper. Many others would feel they had a common interest with the machine and will stop, shop or talk.

33. Make sure you have any required licenses and tax numbers. Check ahead, some localities have strange laws.

34. Can you secure your goods at night? Or do you have to take them down, pack them up and bring them back the next day?

35. If you have come from another area, have you made plans to stay overnight?

36. Does your display protect your items from the hands of small children? They are naturally going to handle your goods.

37. One of the best ways to stop a potential customer is to WEAR A SMILE and give a cheery greeting.

FLEA MARKETS

A lot of people get their start at a flea market. Probably because it is low cost and easy to set up. Here are a few thoughts on the matter:

1. Most items are low cost or second hand. This makes it hard to sell a quality craft/sewing item.

2. If your product can be made in a large volume and for a moderate cost your might have a chance. We have visited dozens of these markets and they run from "junk groups," to some pretty good vendors. The higher quality shows should be classified as "craft shows."

3. Visit as many flea markets as you can BEFORE making a commitment. You can feel the difference. Many are held at drive-in theaters and parking lots. The outdoor ones are usually of lower quality. Then there are the permanent flea markets. There is one in Lake Worth, Florida that has been in existence for about 50 years. Many participants have been there for a long time.
NOTE: One exhibitor makes bride and holiday dolls. She sews and produces them as fast as she can. They are a beautiful creation, and have been very successful. Her husband is her helper and they occupy a permanent booth at this Farmer's Market in Lake Worth, Florida.

4. Find out if the marketeers price-dicker with customers or allow their prices to be discounted.

5. Some markets start at 6:00 in the morning. You may have to be there earlier to obtain a choice location. Many of the choice spots go to regular vendors.

6. Be prepared for the sun, rain, snow, etc. if it is outside. (Follow the suggestions under the previous chapter on craft shows etc.)

7. These shows are good TESTS for you, especially if other vendors have products like yours. Some flea markets handle second hand and junk items. Stay away from these.

CHAPTER 13
PRICING THE PRODUCT

The cost to produce a product can include some or all of the following:

> Time to produce (yours and whoever helps)
> Material
> Marketing (advertising)
> Legal, insurance
> Equipment (sewing machine, typewriter etc.)
> Labels, printing
> Packaging/shipping
> Utilities, phone, lights, electric
> Dues, organizations, newsletters etc.
> Instruction books, manuals, seminars etc.
> Rent or part of house expense

Add these up, then divide by the total amount of products. Shocking! Let's say your monthly expenses are $150 and you have made ten items. That means that each item COSTS $15 to produce. As you produce more the expenses will remain constant and your cost will be lower.

Wilma Brewster of Madison, Wisconsin makes quilted bedspreads and pillows. She found that shipping the bedspreads costs more than the materials. Dorothy Robbins (Stockton, N.Y.) makes a beautiful JINX doll. She cannot find an affordable way to market her creation. Lois Constantino of Riviera Beach, Florida makes a soft doll — like the Cabbage Patch Kid. She is getting $45 to $100 per doll. She can't make them fast enough. She puts them on consignment in various gift and craft stores.

You can do all kinds of figuring, but ultimately you have to research other products such as yours. Inspect sources and compare prices such as:

1. Flea markets, fairs
2. Retail outlets
3. Craft/sewing magazines and books
4. Libraries
5. Newsletters
6. Auctions
7. Ask a friend what it is worth, or better yet a stranger

TIME . . . Many of us probably begin by making about 35¢ an hour. We do have an advantage though. We may create or sew while we are watching TV, waiting for an appointment, listening or carying on a conversation, riding in a car, bus, train, plane, motorcycle, boat etc. This is taking advantage of the precious time we have.

Allan keeps a book in his car. When he comes to a bridge-up, a train, or is waiting to pick up someone, he uses this "FOUND" time to read. He averages an extra book or two a year.

MATERIAL . . . Use the actual price you paid, wholesale or retail. IF you are a frequent customer, ask for a discount. The worst that can happen is that they will say No!.,

MARKETING . . . This is the expensive part of doing business. You should budget so much money and not go beyond.

LEGAL, INSURANCE . . . You may need the help of a lawyer, (such as corporation papers) BUT try to stay away if you can. Most homeowners policies will cover your needs if you stay in the home. If you rent a store THEN it can be a big expense.

EQUIPMENT . . . List and include the costs of all the equipment you use. You may use this as a deduction when filing income taxes. LET'S HOPE you have to file 'cause this means you are selling and making money!

LABELS, PRINTING . . . Each of your creations should have a label with your name, address, price and logo on it.

PACKAGING . . . This includes boxes, tape, mailing labels and postage.

UTILITIES . . . If you use your home and have a designated area for your business and use it JUST for that you may deduct a proportionate amount of your bills. Ask your accountant. It usually is not worth it BECAUSE it turns on a RED LIGHT for the IRS to examine your books.

DUES, ORGANIZATIONS . . . All of this can be and should be an expense.

INSTRUCTION BOOKS, MANUALS, SEMINARS . . . ALL can be part of your costs and can be deducted.

RENT . . . If you have a store of your own or if you use part of your rental house this is a deductible expense.

CHAPTER 14
PACKAGING THE PRODUCT

One of the most important aspects of presenting your creation to the public is the way it is packaged. It has to be able to be packaged for displaying, mailing or shipping in an economical way. It MUST be put in a display that will appeal to the consumer. How many times have you bought a product because of its attractive packaging?

To be attractive to the customer — this is one of the most important steps in manufacturing and marketing. There are many inferior products in quality packaging. We don't mean to say that your product is inferior, but the opposite could happen: a quality product in shabby inferior packaging.

The toy companies have done a great job in packaging so the consumer WANTS to buy the product. The make-up/cosmetic industry have coaxed us to buy with their attractive packaging. Take a look at the periodicals at the supermarket check-out counter *(The National Enquirer, Globe* etc.) their packaging, or cover, is inviting. The product should be placed in a see-thru cellophane/plastic bag on a see-thru box cover. An attractive box will help sell. The packages should have printed material to ex-

Ajax CORP.

PACKAGING PRODUCTS

plain what is inside. You can have attractive labels Xeroxed and stapled to the end of the bag or container. If it is a dress or coat the packaging is more difficult. Do a lot of research. You can examine similar products on the market and STEAL ideas from them. If you are displaying at a show or fair you must make the decision whether or not to package. Many customers like to touch, feel and smell before they buy. Here are a few suggestions for packaging supplies.

1. **MAILING LABELS** . . . You can buy unprinted in stationery stores, for printed consult the numerous office supply sources. (Listed are some good ones; write away for their catalogs.)

> NEBS — 500 Maine St., Groton, Mass 01471.
> THE BUSINESS BOOK — One West Eighth Ave., Oshkosh, WI 54901.
> THE STATIONERY HOUSE — 1000 Florida Ave., Hagerstown, MD 21741.
> THE DRAWING BOARD — 256 Regal Row, Box 220505, Dallas, TX 75222.

> **TAPE** . . . use strapping or special sealing tape if mailing packages.

> **SCALE** . . . Pick up an inexpensive one in the dime store to weigh small packages.

2. **MAILING SCALE** . . . Pitney Bowes rents a machine that will dispense postage as you need it. Ask you post office. (You can buy a small scale for weighing for about $5.00.)

3. **POSTAGE** . . . Check with your post office and see if you can ship 2nd or 4th class and save money. KEEP RECORDS OF ALL YOUR SHIPMENTS — pay a little extra and ask for "**Certificate of Mailing**" form. (See example). Check with the post office about the "official" size and weight requirements. The USP is CHEAPER than UPS for packages under the 50 to 70-pound limits. Heavier than that and you will have to get a trucking company.

U.S. POSTAL SERVICE
CERTIFICATE OF MAILING

Received From

Affix
postage and
postmark. Inquire of
Postmaster for postage

One piece of ordinary mail addressed to

MAY BE USED FOR DOMESTIC AND INTERNATIONAL MAIL. DOES NOT PROVIDE
FOR INSURANCE — POSTMASTER
PS FORM 3817
MAY 1976
*U S GOVERNMENT PRINTING OFFICE 1983 - 754 216

4. **MAILING ENVELOPES** . . . Padded shipping bags (office supply catalogs or stores).

5. **CARTONS AND BOXES** . . . Yellow Pages under corrugated boxes.

NOTE: If you expect to mail out over twelve pieces, consider buying shipping materials in dozens or 50s. You will save quite a bit of money. Call your local phone company for all major cities' Yellow Pages under your area code. They are free. Obtain the major city Yellow Pages — N.Y., Chicago, Los Angeles — for a nominal fee. The phone company will bend over backwards to get these for you. That's what the Yellow Pages are for, BUYING and SELLING.

6. **LABELS** . . . All of these stationery houses have imprinted labels. You can buy 250 or 500 for $20-$30. They will be pressure sensitive on a roll. Ask for a label holder FREE with your order. You may want to start by buying plain unimprinted labels.

7. **PRICE TAGS** . . . Bows, gift labels, price tags, wrapping paper, string, ribbon, imprinted bags, — catalog, Gaylord Specialties, 225 5th Ave., N.Y., N.Y. 10010.

8. **ORDER BOOKS** . . . You can get a "generic" pad from your office supply store, until you can purchase them imprinted (again form the catalogs mentioned).

NOTE: When you start out it is expensive to get items imprinted. BUT it gives the look of professionalism, just like typing instead of handwriting communications.

9. **RECORD KEEPING** . . . Separate yourself from the amateurs and document everything. You will have a more profitable business with efficient records. Here is an idea for your shipping and sales. Record, improve, delete, add or whatever but start one!

Invoice #	Product	Amount	Price	Shipping Cost	Date Rcvd.	Date Shpd.	Shipping Cost
_____	ETC ETC.						

10. **POSTAL CHANGES** . . . Make a decision whether to include shipping charges in the price of your product, charge the customer or add a specific amount. (Example: when we ship a book we charge $1/book for shipping and handling.)

NOTE: We repeat — SAVE all postage receipts, mark on them what, where and when you shipped. A customer might say they never received it OR it could be lost. You must have proof of mail-

ing. If you have a valuable product, insure it or use "Certificate of Mailing". You may buy a set of postage stampers — FRAGILE, RETURN, POSTAGE GUARANTEE etc. at your office supply store. Make sure you use the appropriate packaging materials or the USP will not accept.

11. **YOUR ADDRESS . . .** There have been many opinions about addresses. Many say that a box number makes the customer feel suspicious about how bona fide the company is. Other say it saves a lot of unnecessary phone calls etc. We personally prefer the genuine address AND give our phone number for anyone to call. Get a P.O. Box number to test new products, ads and inquiries. When we wanted an illustrator, we used a P.O. box number to prevent phone calls and visits. We received over 100 inquiries. Some were very persistent and a few were indignant because they were writing to A. Smith at a post office box.

CHAPTER 15
CONSIGNMENTS

Here are some PROs and CONs of consigning products (putting your creation in a retail store without charging the owner UNTIL it is sold).

1. For the beginner it might be the ONLY way to get started.

2. Consign them ONLY to shoppes that you can physically visit.

3. Many stores change owners or go out of business. Be careful.

4. Your creation may very well be damaged or soiled.

5. Who pays for stolen merchandise?

6. Whose insurance covers fire, flood etc. damage? Legally the product is still yours.

7. Will the store owner display and promote YOUR creation over their own or one with a greater profit margin?

8. You cannot give a better profit to consigned goods. You are the risk taker. We have seen 20 to 33% discount on consigned goods, any more is approaching desperation.

9. Your record-keeping is increased.

10. You physically have to follow up for reorders or returns.

11. You are tying up a lot of capital (money) by LENDING your product to a store.

12. There are some successful area craft stores that can do wonders with your creation. Visit them and become friends.

13. A good rule of thumb — if the shop is over two years old you know they are successful. **(MANY RETAIL BUSINESSES FAIL WITHIN 10 MONTHS).** There are the 10% that become winners. Start small with a few items, then leave more if they sell.

Sara Addington from Birmingham, Georgia tells us that the only way she got started in her store was with consigned goods. She started with 15 or 20 products and now has over 200. Once she had proved herself, the craft people just poured in with their products.

14. There is some "shoddy merchandise" being made. You will have to sell the "quality" of your sewing creation.

15. It helps to have a printed price list. (Type it and have it photocopied for pennies OR have it typeset and printed for still a nominal fee. Example:

	one color	two color	three	four
Designer Pillow (small)	$12.00	15.00	17.50	22.50
Designer Pillow (medium)	15.00	17.50	22.50	25.00
Designer Pillow (large)	17.50	22.50	25.00	27.50
Designer Pillow (king)	22.50	25.00	27.50	30.00

Three or more . . . . less 10%
Six or more . . . . less 20%
Twelve or more . . . . less 33%

WE ACCEPT MASTER/VISA & PERSONAL CHECKS (U.S. funds)
PHONE ORDERS!! 1-800-111-2222

SHIPPING CHARGE — add $2 to each pillow
ALL ORDERS SHIPPED WITHIN FIVE WORKING DAYS

100% SATISFACTION GUARANTEED. If not completely satisfied send back (prepaid) undamaged goods for full refund.

NOTE: NOTICE U.S. funds only. If you get foreign money orders and checks paid in their country's funds you will be a loser IF their currency is less than ours. (Example: Canadian funds can cost you up to 25% less.)

PERSONAL CHECKS . . . We have found in the many years in business that we have been "stuck" with only 3 or 4 checks out of the hundreds we have processed. It seems that craft and mail order people are above average in honesty.

I would strongly suggest a BLACK & WHITE photo of your product(s). A colored imprinted price list will cost more.

16. Have a consignment form and get everything in writing (NOT VERBAL). There are still some people who do business with a handshake; you may be able to someday also but until then CYA (Cover Your A--). GET IT IN WRITING. If you offer one shop a different deal than another write it on the consignment form.

NAME OF RETAIL SHOP_____

ADDRESS _____TELEPHONE _____

STATE_____ZIP_____OWNER_____

CONSIGNING COMPANY/PERSON _____

ADDRESS_____PHONE _____

This agreement is between the shop and craftperson listed above.

DATE OF PLACEMENT ____PERIOD OF TIME _____

RETAIL PRICE _____WHOLESALE COST _____

1. The retail price of the product will not be discounted.

2. The Consigning Company agrees to pick up any UN-DAMAGED products at the end of this agreement or at RENEWAL of the Consignment Time.

3. The store owner is responsible for any theft or damage to the consigned product.

4. The Consigning Company will be paid for sold merchandise every thirty days, at the end of the agreement or whichever comes first.

Item	Retail Price	Store Profit	Due Consignor	Date Paid

_____Etc. Etc.

SIGNER RETAILER _____

    CONSIGNER_____**DATE**_____

NOTE: *Just read in Sunday's paper about a gal who specializes. She makes matching coats, boots and sunglasses for DOGS. She caters to the above-average pet owner, the Palm Beachers etc. Some have ordered up to twenty different costumes for their "mutts." She has even made tuxedos and formal gowns. Isn't this a great country! What opportunity for those who have imagination, persistence and desire.*

CHAPTER 16
SELLING BY MAIL

This is one of the fastest-growing segments of American business. With two in the family working and the emphasis being on leisure time activities, shopping-by-mail is the answer. The future home computers will increase this a great deal. Let's take a look at the pluses and minuses before we make a decision on selling by mail.

DISADVANTAGES

- Compiling a mailing list can be time consuming and tedious.

- Buying a prepared mailing list can be expensive and does not guarantee accuracy.

- Preparing promotional pieces such as brochures, price lists, catalogs and slingers is an art and takes time, talent and money.

SELLING BY MAIL (MAIL ORDER) . . . Selling by mail is defined as using the mail to promote, sell and/or distribute a product, book, business, idea, politics etc.

DIRECT MAIL . . . means sending your product or service by mail. The customer could originate from a magazine ad, a sign, or word of mouth etc.

- You never come in contact with people you are selling.

- Your reputation builds on promotional materials, not on your personality, looks or sparkling conversation.

- You have to depend on the erratic U.S. Postal System.

- You have no control on the timing and delivery of your mail.

- Response for money-promotions (asking the customer to send a check for the merchandise) is excellent at 1-2% of the total amount of mailings.

- Attrition (people moving, dying, disappearing) is now at 25%. That means that on any mailing list that is a year old, 25% are not at that address. If you mail 4th class, there are no forwarding privileges, thus 1/4 of your mailing pieces go into the round file (garbage).

ADVANTAGES

- It requires very little initial investment.

- It can be operated full or part time.

- Can be operated at home.

- No large amount of stock has to be warehoused.

- No high rent, wages, expenses have to be incurred.

- You eliminate all middleman, distributor, wholesaler and retailer profits.

- You are working for yourself. If you don't want to work you don't have to, you can work in the middle of the night, take a nap or whatever.

- You can't get fired and you are starting at the top.

- Your business will grow if you have persistence and desire.

NOTE: *Richard W. Sears started selling low priced watches by mail. He was fairly successful when he merged with A.C. Roebuck and expanded into jewelry. They added more merchandise and sent out a catalog. You know the rest of the story.*

There have been hundreds of books written on the mail order business. This is not one of them. We will try to outline the important aspects of selling by mail.

You may want to pick up a few books on mail order. We found that researching and reading saved us a lot of money and time, especially when we started writing books. Others have been there and have made the same mistakes. A successful person learns by OTHERS' mistakes, not by his own. Here are some books that may help before you enter this "way of doing business."

- *How to Avoid the 22 Costly Mistakes on Mail Order* — Buchanan c/o Towers Club, Box 2038-S, Vancouver, WA 98668-2038.

- *How to Sell Information by Mail Successfully* — D'Aquila. He didn't put his address in the book. Now I can't pass it on to you. LESSON . . . make sure you have your name or company name on EVERYTHING you send out. Even 2 or 3 times is not enough.

- *How Mail Order Fortunes are Made* — Arco, 219 Park Ave. S., N.Y., N.Y. 10003.

- *Building a Mail Order Business* — Cohen 1556 Sierra Padre, Pasadena, CA 91107.

Check your library for other sources. PLEASE do some reading and question asking BEFORE you start. We have seen people lose tens of thousands of dollars in this business by being too impulsive. Many have made fortunes in the mail order business, you can too. Do a lot of preparing and planning.

NOTE: *The BEST way to use a mailing list is to create your own. It will take a little time BUT it will be yours forever. If you "rent" a list you can only use it once. You have no idea how old or accurate it is. In our experience, and we are not the final word, stay away from the "List Houses." They will charge you $40-60 per thousand, sometimes with a five thousand limit.*

HOW TO CREATE YOUR OWN LIST

1. **SAVE, COLLECT** and **FILE** all of your customers' names and addresses.

2. You may have a computer company store these names/addresses for you OR put them on your own home computer.

3. Find sewing books, magazines, and newsletters. Copy the names and addresses of the advertisers and add these to your list (especially the classified).

4. Write to these same publications and ask if they rent their lists.

5. Find a small operator as you are and share lists.

6. Share your list when it gets to five thousand or more with another larger operator or publication.

7. Don't be afraid of entering your relatives' and friends' names.

8. Find out the kinds of products sell the best when sold by mail.

9. Remember that finished products that have to be seen by eye or impulse are difficult to sell by mail. Its description must be easily put into words or into a picture or drawing.

© SEWING FOR PROFIT

"I GET THE FEELING THAT MRS. GOTROCKS PAID HER SEWING BILL!"

CHAPTER 17
SELLING PATTERNS

Where do all of these wonderful designed clothes, accessories and assorted items originate? Big pattern companies solicit and buy 85% of their patterns from independent artists such as you. If you have developed a pattern, you have the option of selling it yourself just as you would any other creation or product.

1. At craft shows, fairs, flea markets, etc.
2. To retail and craft stores
3. By direct mail
4. Advertising in magazines, newletters, newspapers, etc.
5. At your home by operating your own sale
6. Selling direct to magazines

We all would like to sell our original designs to one of the needlecraft publications. It's like selling anything else to anyone else. You have to do your homework first and realize WHAT to do before the rejection slips come in. Here are some tips.

1. Is your design original or an adaptation of another?

2. Have you used a new technique or involve the use of new materials?

3. Have you written clear instructions? IF not have someone who is good at writing help you do it!

4. Test your instructions with a student to determine if they can be followed easily. IF they have completed it with few questions then you have done well.

5. Have you used standardized abbreviations and simple language?

6. Have you included a list of materials needed with the amount, size, color and brand names?

7. Have you suggested substitutes for the name brands?

8. "A picture is worth a thousand words." Use illustrations, photographs or cartoons to help "sell" your idea and pattern.

9. Use a professional photographer if you are an amateur.

10. Find out the magazine that will fit your product.

11. Make sure you time your selling enough ahead. Christmas items have to have a lead time of about nine months.

12. Send a query letter to the editor with a written description and colored photos (enclosed in plastic folders).

13. Enclose a LSASE.

14. Send the product ONLY when the editor requests.

15. Insure and package securely.

16. Read carefully the contract sent back to you. It will contain a statement to the effect that you certify the project you have submitted is your original work and not previously published. Most will ask for all rights of copyright material. Make sure you understand everything clearly.

17. Understand the payment you will receive.

18. Ask for additional copies of the magazine.

19. Be PROUD of your accomplishment.

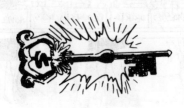

CHAPTER 18
EXPANDING AND DIVERSIFYING

In the business world, the rule is that you cannot remain the same — you either have to increase, expand or go backwards. There is no constant . . . costs, utilities, personal needs and payroll go up. As a result you must increase the volume of business to meet this increase. You reach a point of saturation, when you can sell just so much to so many. You then have to expand your product line, advertising, sales force or area of marketing.

A. WHAT AND HOW DO YOU DO IT?

Let's share some ideas and opportunities:

1. To expand you should be successful with what you are selling now.

2. Examine products that are similar, can enhance or be a companion to yours.

3. Most successful businesses have MULTIPLES to sell. As soon as you feel that your first line of products is selling well, be ready with additional items.

4. Be sure you need that extra person. It means additional record keeping, payroll records, taxes etc. You might be consider-

ing paying them "under the counter" or not taking out taxes. Here are some of the disadvantages of paying without deducting taxes:

    a.   They can become injured on the job and sue you for medical expenses.

    b.   If they become angry or mad at you, they can go to the labor board and "turn you in." This means you could be liable for ALL back taxes AND penalties and interest charges.

    c.   You will not be able to use this payroll expense as a deduction on your income tax report.

    d.   The person has no proof that they ever worked.

    e.   If enough people find out, others may "blow the whistle on you."

5. You may employ two or less people and not have to take out workman's compensation.

6. When you put that extra person(s) to work, DON'T give away your business secrets. I have seen many "copy cats," those who STEAL ideas from others while they are working. One of our friends, Jerry Buchanan of the Towers Club Newsletter, advises that as soon as we publish a book we should promote it like mad. He states that there are many who will steal or copy a successful book.

7. When we were in the pharmacy business Allan learned from an old wise druggist something that has lasted in our minds for years. "NEVER LET THEM KNOW BUSINESS IS GOOD, SOMEONE WILL OPEN ACROSS THE STREET FROM YOU. TELL THEM 'IT COULD BE BETTER'." It's hard not to brag or tell the world of your successes BUT it pays to keep it to yourself or to your trusted loved ones.

8. You don't need **partners,** you need **helpers!**

9. Test any added ideas BEFORE investing a lot of time and money.

10. Construct a procedure plan, a budget and a projected sales estimate.

11. Do you have enough capital, expertise, equipment, finances and time to do a good job?

12. Do your homework and prepare well.

B. DIFFERENT AREAS OF SEWING

Dolls
Doll clothing   Costumes
Pet clothing   Square dancing costumes

Women's clothes	Vests
Negligees and "sexy" under-garments	Placemats and napkins
Robes, House coats	Western and English riding apparel
Men's ties	Christmas ornaments, wreaths, dolls, placemats
Embroidery	
Monograms on shirts, towels, etc.	Tee shirts, etc.
Stuffed animals	Valentine items
Pillows	Easter items
Drapes/curtains	Mother's Day items
Alterations	Father's Day items
Slipcovers	Fall/Halloween items
Bedspreads	Sewing machine repair
Comforters	Teaching sewing
	Writing a book on sewing

Success Stories

Jay Van Andel and Richard DeVos started marketing products from a small store in 1959. They have made it together in a "rare" partnership operation. Today their partnership has expanded to an over one billion dollar company. They call it Amway.

Steven Job and Steve Wozniak started making computers in Steve's garage about seven years ago. They still are together and have moved from the garage to much larger quarters. They call their company "Apple Computer."

Mary Crowley was recruited from a furniture store to work for Stanley Home Products. The gal who lured her away was named Mary Kay. She started a business of her own called Mary Kay Cosmetics. Mary Crowley then started her own decorative gifts with her $6,000 savings. She used the Tupperware party method of selling her goods in 1957. Today her company does $400 million, has 40,000 managers and sales people and produces a profit of $40 million. The name of the company — Home Interiors and Gifts Inc.

C. TYPES OF BUSINESS STRUCTURES

As you grow you must hire other people. You will first need someone to handle the "paper" work — the bills, incoming monies, the payroll and the books. You might need a salesper-son or a mail room person. You may consider changing from an individual form of business to a "partnership" or a corporation.

WE STRONGLY ADVISE **NOT** TO GO INTO A PARTNER-SHIP. In all of my (Allan's) businesses and consulting "I have seen hundreds of partnerships. I don't think six of them are still in business as the original partnership or are the partners talking

92

to one another. I had a consulting job in one of the New England States. Two brothers owned the business, a distribution company. They had been in partnership for over forty years. For the last twenty years one brother would pick up the other one at his house at 7:00 each morning. They would return at the end of the day at 5:00. During those twenty years they had NEVER spoken a word to each other. They had had a fight and neither forgave the other. I could cite many examples of "bad" marriages such as this, and that is what a partnership is . . . a marriage.

LOOK INTO A SUBCHAPTER S CORPORATION . . . it is taxed like an individual business but has the advantages of a corporation. Here are some comparisons from a U.S. LABOR DEPT. booklet.

ADVANTAGES	DISADVANTAGES

Individual Proprietorship

ADVANTAGES	DISADVANTAGES
1. Controlled by owner	1. Liability unlimited
2. All profits to owner	2. Limited rersources
3. Little regulation	3. No continuity at retirement or death
4. Easy to start	
5. Earnings personally taxes	

General Partnership

ADVANTAGES	DISADVANTAGES
1. Joint ownership and responsibility	1. Conflict of authority
2. Access to more money and skills	2. Liability unlimited
3. Earnings personally taxed	3. Profits divided
4. Limited regulation and easy to start	4. No continuity at retirement or death

Limited Partnership

ADVANTAGES	DISADVANTAGES
1. General partner(s) run the business	1. Limited partners have no say in business
2. Limited (silent) partners have no liability beyond invested money	2. General partners have unlimited liability
3. Profits divided as per partnership agreement	3. More regulations to start than general partnership
4. Earnings personally taxed	

Corporation

ADVANTAGES	DISADVANTAGES
1. Limited liability	1. Regulated by states
2. Ownership interest in transferrable	2. Costly to form
3. Legal entity and continuous life	3. Limited to chartered activities

4. Status in raising funds	4. Corporate income tax plus tax on personal salary and/or dividends

Subchapter S Corporations

1. Receives all advantages of a corporation	1. Highly regulated both by state and IRS
2. Electing corporation taxed as sole proprietorship	2. Restricted to certain kinds of business and limited number of stockholders

D. RUNNING A HOME SHOW OR CRAFT BOUTIQUE

Many of you are familiar with the various types of Home Shows or "Party Plan" selling. The original was probably Tupperware. Since then you can find candy, toys, feminine ware, books, Christmas goods, baked goods and numerous other products that are sold in a "party" atmosphere at someone's home. What is stopping you?

In the 8/23/83 issue of *Family Circle* there is an article by Gerri Hirshey. It's called "Beyond Garage Sales: The Home Boutique." A couple of gals got about 20 exhibitors in a Chicago suburb and had a Christmas boutique called "The Stuffed Stocking." They pooled their time and money, got together groups of craftpeople for $20 per exhibitor and held the show in one of their homes. It has been documented that some of these home shows have been known to gross up to $10,000 in a two-day period. These shows are great follow-ups for the rest of the year and for repeat selling. To produce a Christmas show takes a lot of preparing, probably starting in the spring. Mailing lists, brochures, exhibitors, and crafts have to be prepared.

Here are some suggestions IF you decide to put one on:

1. Decide on the date.

2. Make out a Master Plan and Procedure Chart.

3. Determine if you want to be the boss and organizer.

4. If you decide to go into this venture with others, hold your first meeting.

5. Designate responsibilities — a chairperson, treasurer, secretary, advertising chairman, craft evaluation person etc.

6. Start with enough time to prepare.

7. Choose a name.

8. Choose the home and the area to be used.

9. Select the types of crafts or sewing items to display.

10. If you are running it yourself, decide on the mark-up for the product, how much YOUR profit will be.

11. Search out other individual craft and sewing people who can and will participate.

12. Determine an amount you will charge for each participant to display their goods.

13. Prepare an advertising brochure (either sell ads or include it in your fee to the participants).

14. Obtain mailing lists to send your advertisement.

15. Decide if you want to advertise, where, how long, how much and when. You should have an advertising budget and a projection of sales. Example:

If you have 20 exhibitors and they pay $30 a person then you will have $600 to promote and prepare. Your profit will be from the commission you will receive. If 20 exhibitors sell $200 each and you take 20% your profit will be 20 x $200 = $4,000. . .20% will be $800.

16. You can run these at different times of the year — Valentine's Day, Easter, Mother's Day, Father's Day, Thanksgiving, Halloween — any time that will give you a good reason to have a home show.

17. Make sure every customer's address is received for the next show's mailing list.

18. Follow the directions as you would for a craft or garage sale.

19. Have price lists and discount policies predetermined.

20. If you are running the show, then YOU collect all monies.

21. Have a system to credit the right craftperson the correct amount. Usually a triple label, one for the customer, one for the exhibitor and one for you or the money collector is used.

22. Serve coffee, teas, soft drinks etc. to help the consumer stay longer. Background music and a COOL room will make them buy more. If a room is too warm people tend to leave faster.

23. Decorate your display area appropriately.

24. Deduct, record and pay the required taxes. SOMEONE will notice if you do not!

25. Make sure all exhibitors have ENOUGH products to meet the demand.

26. You should demand to receive commissions on special

and pending orders.

IF YOU HAVE A REPUTATION FOR HONEST DEALINGS AND FOR LARGE CROWDS YOU WILL HAVE PLENTY OF PARTICIPANTS. You will probably have to turn some down. If you grow large enough you may have to move to larger rented display areas.

E. RUNNING A GARAGE SEWING/CRAFT SALE

1. Purchase a book (paperback $2-3) on how to run a garage sale.

2. Determine where you will hold it.

3. Determine whose stuff you'll be selling.

NOTE: *By just asking friends, neighbors, and relatives you will be able to find other craft items to sell. Offer to pay them 25-40% of the sale price.*

4. Construct signs. A pole and a piece of scrap plywood OR cardboard will do.

5. If you are not a good printer, find someone to do it for you, for nothing of course.

6. Include on the signs: Garage Sale, date, time and place.

7. Place the sign anywhere there is traffic. Ask the corner gas station owner, put paper signs on bulletin boards —

ANYWHERE it will bring people to your sale.

8. Be sure and put a small ad in the Penny Saver.

9. Indicate the time, usually 8:00 a.m. to 1:00 Saturday and Sunday. People will come the day before and even ring the bell at 6:00 a.m. Dealers and bargain hunters will be the first to arrive, ready to grab a bargain.

10. Find tables that will display the merchandise.

11. Put anything out. You'll be surprised — the oddest things will sell.

12. Buy price tags and price everything. Price about 50% of the retail value.

13. Put some price on all things.

14. Be prepared to move inside in case of rain.

NOTE: *DO NOT, DO NOT allow anyone inside your home for any reason while you are selling — for obvious reasons.*

15. Have bags and newspapers to wrap items.

16. Have about $50 in change. You don't want to lose a sale because of a lack of it. Get a roll each of pennies, dimes, nickels, quarters and the rest in $1 bills.

WHAT TO DO DURING THE SALE

DO have help, especially to watch for shoplifters and price tag switchers.

DO have music from radio or stereo. Not loud rock! Most of your customers will be middle-to-old-agers. They will be turned off by modern music. You want to encourage the customer to stay longer and to put into your paw the green stuff. It has been proven that people will stay longer and buy more with music in the background.

DO be prepared to dicker. This is the American Garage Sale Way . . . "Try to get it for less!"

DO block off the driveway to prevent traffic jams. Yes, a lot of people will come if you use these simple rules.

NOTE: *You can run these sales for other people on their property with their goods. I would suggest that you take a 25-40% fee of the sale price.*

DO keep your money and change on your person. There are always a few who will steal anything.

DO lock your house or apartment door if no one is inside while you are outside.

DO act friendly. You will meet a lot of neighbors and people who could become good friends.

DO mark everything so there will not be any question.

DO let your kids, grand-kids, neighbors' kids sell Kool-Aid or lemonade OR set them up and take a piece of the action.

DON'T expect to sell everything. Some people give the rest to charity or combine it with another person's sale OR keep it until the next one.

AFTER THE SALE IS OVER

1. Put all the unsold goods back where they belong.

2. Remove price tags and signs from where you put them.

3. Clean the area.

4. Make notes to yourself. This will help you improve and remember how to do it again.

A GREAT "ego-pacifier" . . . having your shirt, towel, shorts, tie, etc. monogrammed with your initials or name.

F. MONOGRAMMING

SUCCESS STORIES

Don Short of North Palm Beach, The Monogram Shop, started monogramming friends' shirts and found that many others also wanted it done. He also found that stores such as Sears, Penneys, Burdines etc. sold towels that needed initial monogramming. He soon had all their business and more than he could handle. He was working 16 hours per day to catch up. He has purchased a computer monogramming machine to speed up the initialing.

In the April '83 issue of *INC* magazine they tell the story of Mark Kaufman who started out monogramming corporate logos and last year grossed (brought in) $1 million in sales. Some of his clients are PepsiCo., United Airlines, Mobil Oil. He is now working on a "Gentlemen's Designer Collection" for Johnny Walker Black Label Scotch whiskey, including a monogrammed rugby shirt, a warm up shirt, a V-neck sweater and a garment bag.

We repeat, "The sweetest sound in any man's language is the sound (or sight) of his own name." Here is a great way to capitalize on this fact. You can do it by hand at first, then purchase a used or new sewing machine that can be adapted to this craft.

At holiday time a great idea is to **SELL** and monogram towels etc.

RECOMMENDATIONS

1. Distribute your slingers or brochures to area department stores, sewing stores and places where women will see them (they will probably be your best customers) for towels etc. Men love to have their shirts monogrammed.

2. Make up a sample of a monogrammed shirt (women's and men's), towel and guest towel to show.

3. Have an artist friend (if you cannot), draw a picture of your samples for your slinger.

4. Establish a price list.

Towels (three types of styles)	$ 2.75 each
Guest towels	2.50 each
Shirts, shorts	2.50 each

5. Put the samples in a plastic sealed bag. This will prevent them from becoming soiled from so much handling.

6. Have references by doing some for friends or not-the-same-name relative.

7. Realize that after you have sold a few, others will come knocking at your door, ESPECIALLY if they are done well.

8. Have an order pad and receipt book.

9. Ask for deposit IF you are selling the towel etc.

10. Take an inventory, in writing, of the terms that you will be taking to monogram.

11. Triple check the initials that are to be sewn for correctness.

12. Have 3 or 4 different styles of letters from which to pick.

13. Give a date of completion and honor the date.

14. Insist on complete payment on delivery.

15. Investigate the possibility of obtaining business from retailer.

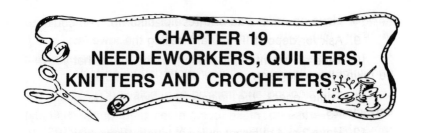

CHAPTER 19
NEEDLEWORKERS, QUILTERS,
KNITTERS AND CROCHETERS

There are over 50 million of you in the United States; 42% of you are selling or want to sell your creation(s). Some are saying "Why sell mine, when so many want to do it themselves." Good statement, but not good enough to stop a smart businessperson.

1. You can teach others to master what you have learned. Craft stores are always looking for instructors.

2. Sell patterns to others or to shops.

3. Make hand-painted canvases. BE CREATIVE AND IMAGINATIVE!!

4. Embroidery kits are in big demand.

5. Make custom-designed and hand-made eyeglass holders and sell them to eyeglass stores.

6. Design and make belts and sell them to dress shops.

7. Make and sell handbags to area women's shops.

8. Hats are coming back. Use your imagination.

9. A gal in the West Palm Beach Mall hand paints and

designs names on umbrellas. She's cleaning up. You could do the same thing with needle and thread.

10. Find a place that sells sweaters, ties, pillow cases, men's and somen's shirts and sell your monogramming talent.

11. Sell blocking and framing of needlework.

12. Advertise to make custom-designed quilts. I (Judy) remember that when I was a kid, my Mother gave each one of us a quilt for our bed with gigantic initials on each. We had those until they were threads. Everyone loves to see their name or facsimile on something.

13. Crocheted items are tough to sell, but how-to manuals and instructions are always saleable. Magazines are hungry for stories on how-to and crocheting articles are always popular.

14. Remember the hand-made sweaters with the deer-heads on them when we were teenagers? They are coming back. You might advertise and sell a hand-made original.

CHAPTER 20
TEACHING, WRITING AND LECTURING

TEACHING

The expression of one's talent comes out in different ways. Some can sew, some sell well, others are good businesspeople. A lot have all of these attributes and them some.

A great way to sharpen your skills and find new methods and ideas is to teach a course on your skill. Community Adult Education departments in public and private schools are searching for people to teach others. We have done this for years and find it very rewarding. High schools and colleges enroll as many in their Adult Education courses as they do in the regular school programs. You may be able to teach at the YMCA and Senior Citizen centers.

The pay is pretty good, but the great benefit is from the friends you will meet and the ideas that are exchanged. Do you remember the CETA government program that had sewing instructors to help the unemployed and unemployable learn new skills?

Here are some suggestions:

1. Attend a class and find out how they function. Most are very informal and interesting.

2. Put a program together: Quilting, Soft Doll Making, How to make Patterns, Christmas Gift Making with a Needle and Thread, How to Sell Your sewing Creations etc.

3. Make it a 4-5 week program of 2-2½ hours each.

4. Start with the basics, then get into specific ideas.

NOTE: A lot of the classes taught, use workbooks. This should be carefully put together, photocopied, stapled together. You may charge extra for these guides. If it is well done, every class member will buy one. If you have 20 in class and you sell it for $10, that's an added $200 in your pocket.

5. DON'T LECTURE. Share ideas and allow input from the class members.

6. ALLOW THEM TO MAKE SOMETHING with their hands. This will give them tangible evidence of their talent.

7. REMEMBER these students are great additions to your mailing list and possible customers for your products.

8. Your reputation will spread like wildfire IF you know how to relate to others. You don't have to be a polished public speaker or a professional teacher. IF you have the intelligence and crativeness to make things then you can tell and teach others.

9. The more you teach, the more your confidence will grow.

10. You might teach in TANDEM with another person who is involved in the same kind of sewing. This will DOUBLE the effectiveness of your program.

11. ALWAYS ask for and retain participants' names and addresses.

12. Pass out a questionaire at the end of the last class:

NAME OF CLASS _____

INSTRUCTOR _____

DATE _____ TIME _____ PLACE _____

WHAT DID YOU ENJOY THE MOST? _____

WHAT COULD BE IMPROVED ON? _____

WHAT OTHER CLASS OF THIS KIND WOULD YOU LIKE TO HAVE? _____

Let them leave off their names. It will give a more constructive evaluation of your efforts. It is no fun to have negative feedback BUT if you accept it and improve, then you are the winner.

13. Don't be afraid to use the blackboard of visual aids if you have access to them.

WRITING

1. **Articles to magazines, newsletters, newspapers etc.**

There are a few sewing craft people who supplement their incomes by writing and selling articles. Where do you think a lot of these magazines get their news? Much of it comes from free lance writers.

1. Do some research and write about what you do or know WELL!

2. Make a rough outline of your idea.

3. Determine which magazine you want to sell it to. YOU SHOULD ONLY SUBMIT THE ARTICLE TO ONE SOURCE AT A TIME.

4. Get several issues and examine the style of writing and the types of articles. Make a choice that fits your style of writing.

5. Make sure to OFFER the reader something. How will they benefit from the information you are offering?

6. Address the article to the editor or to the proper person, NOT just to the magazine. A janitor or third class typist may get it and throw it away.

7. Buy or consult:
   1) **Writer's Market** — it will list EVERY Major magazine.
   2) **International Directory of Little Magazines and Small Press** — over 4,000 markets for writers — Dustbooks, Box 100, Paradise, Ca. 95969.
   3) **Standard Rate & Data Service; Consumer Magazine** and **Agri-Media Rates & Data** (At your library) includes every magazine published.

8. After you send one article, start with another article. It may take months before you get the rejection or acceptance slip. Keep information on the editor's desk. Soon they will recognize you and your talent.

9. Suggest ideas to editors about which you could write.

10. Magazines etc. buy from experts. Find your notch and keep plugging.

11. Build your information files. Clip and snip everything you read on your subject. Don't be afraid to steal an idea or two from others.

12. Keep a POSITIVE attitude. I (Allan) have talked to writers who have given up after one or two rejections. Writing is much like selling; you have to be able to accept rejection.

2. Writing a book

Everyone wants to write a book and many have the ability and the knowledge, but 99.9% lack the motivation and drive to actually sit down and write the book. One of the most important pieces of advice: WRITING IS 5%, PROMOTING IS 95% of producing a book.

You must have the information on HOW to get it published and sold. I would strongly recommend buying Dan Poynter's book, **The Self Publishing Manual**. It is the best we have read and we have read hundreds of books on the "How to's" of book writing and publishing — Para Publishing, Box 4232-A Santa Barbara, CA 93103-0232.

Your articles could be structured so they consist of a chapter at a time. When you are finished with 15 or 20 articles you have already written a book.

If you have a good manuscript or completed book, write to me and I will give you my opinion. I may publish, promote or sell it for you. Allan Smth, 8084 Nashua Dr., c/o Success Publishing, Lake Park, FL 33410.

LECTURING

Do you have the gift to speak before people? (KNOW WHAT? The biggest fear the human has . . . it's not facing death, it's speaking before people.) BUT if you have the desire and the talent you can make some added monies.

Barbara Brabec of Creative Cash, Dottie Walters of Sharing Ideas newsletters both speak throughout the country. They started with newsletters, articles to magazines, then to their own books, then to the lecture circuit.

You will have to have a good talk or lecture and be able to promote yourself to the various organizations that look for speakers. If you are good, they will seek you out.

CHAPTER 21
SEWING REPAIRS, TAILORING
AND CUSTOM WORK

There are many individuals and retail cleaning shops look-ing for people who can do alterations and repairs. Here are some guidelines:

1. Deteremine what you can and want to do in the line of alterations and repairs.

2. Collect the proper threads, buttons, etc.

3. Decide if you will pick up or have the customer drop off the repairs to you. If you pick up (probably for retail shops) then your price will be higher OR you will charge a pick-up fee.

4. Make out a price list. Example:
Replace buttons . . . .$1.00 per item
Shorten garments . . . .$10.00 per arm/leg
Reshape or restructure . . . .$2.00 per inch
Custom sewing . . . . .upon request

5. Give a claim ticket with each item listed on your copy and the customer's copy.

6. Have plastic garmet bags or other wrapping materials to avoid damage or soiling.

7. Allow so much time for the customer to pick up their repairs THEN warn them that it will be sold or discarded.

8. If you have a lot of unclaimed items, consider charging a deposit.

9. Make sure you and the customer understand exactly what is to be done and how much will be charged.

If you have any ideas, successes or information . . . drop us a line we would love to share it with others. — Love to hear from you.

Judy & Allan Smith
8084 Nashua Dr.
Lake Park, FL 33410

INDEX

WANNA MOTIVATE YOUR TEENAGER TO MAKE MONEY

AMERICAN LIBRARY ASSOCIATION BOOKLIST "REVIEW"

Practical advice and an upbeat approach, in both narrative and format, make this useful for junior high would-be entrepreneurs. BE. Smith is energetic and encouraging in a better-than-average roundup of self-starting business opportunities for ambitious teens. He begins with useful advice on business realities — licensing, self promotion, insurance, bookkeeping, etc. — following up with job profiles that include estimates of set-up costs, along with a wealth of advice on how to do the job and do it well. Fairly familiar businesses are described — gift wrapping, baby-sitting, cake-baking — but the author also suggests a number of innovative ways to turn a profit, among them, conducting home furnishings inventories, lending toys, removing stains from driveways and patios and extracting tree stumps. While Smith doesn't guarantee success, his business hints are sensible suggestions bound to put teenage entrepreneurs on the right track. Decorated with black-and-white cartoon drawings. Junior high and high school.

■ TEENAGE MONEYMAKING GUIDE
— Allan Smith

A book for those who would like to make money on their own. Years of research provides information for 101 money making opportunities. It gives the reader motivation to be a winner in life by being their own boss. The young entrepreneur is shown the possible costs, time, materials and recommendations before, during and after the job is over. The 281 pages are jam-packed with 136 illustrations, 50 actual success stories and 12 basic secrets of business. It has been proven that employed people are benefits to themselves and the community they live in. The F.B.I. states that 33% of major crimes committed in the U.S. are by unemployed teenagers. This guide can help shape productive futures.

WINNER'S MAKE IT HAPPEN, LOSER'S STAND AROUND AND ASK, "WHAT HAPPENED."

Success Publications •
281 pages
L.C. 84-90126
ISBN 0-931113-00-8
Soft Cover $10.00
5½ x 8½

■ HOW TO SELL YOUR HOMEMADE CREATION — Allan Smith

★ 100 Material Sources
★ 18 Ways to Get Free Exposure & Publicity
★ 30 Marketing Areas
★ 100 Potential Buyers
★ How to Test, Price, Pack, Ship, & Manage Your Business

Just published, this is a book for those with talent, for those who have created something they want to show or sell to the world. A guide for those who have to start small and with limited money. Written with twenty years experience in successful home-based and self-marketing businesses. It will walk you through the basics of selling your product to the consumer. Where and how to find free or low cost publicity, how to create an appealing ad, how to name, price, package and mail your product. It lists 25 different market areas and over 100 places that might buy your creation. This 200 page 8½ x 11 manual will save you hours of wasted effort and many dollars in wasted cash. This is the first step when considering going in business for yourself.

Success Publications •
152 pages
L.C. 84-51623
ISBN 0-931113-01-6
Soft Cover $11.95
8½ x 11

■ HOW TO MAKE SCHOOL FUN — Allan H. Smith

This book is for the parent or child that needs help accepting school. 76% of surveyed school children stated that they did not like going to school. Whose fault is it? It could be the school system and it could be the attitude of the parent and/or student. Loaded with chapters on building self confidence, getting acceptance by peers, getting teachers on your side, how to be popular and well-liked. How to turn around those DULL classes, boring teachers, restless bus rides, un-imaginable P.E. classes and tasteless lunches. How to get involved, coordinate work, home and school. How to earn and save money, should I drop out? and much, much more. FINALLY! a book that tells it like it is and how to improve and capitalize on those productive young years of school life.

Success Publications • 200 pages
L.C. 84-90227; ISBN 0-931113-03-2
Soft Cover $10.00; 5½ x 8½

- Getting Teachers on Your Side
- How To Be Well-Liked
- How "To Play The Game"
- Getting To Know You
- Working & School
- Looking Ahead After School Years
- How To Choose A Career

12 Oz. Coffee Mug

Reg. $2.95

Special 2/$5.00

$1.00 Shipping & Handling

I ♥ DOLLS
I Sew Smart
I Sew Great

Bumper Stickers
$1.25 ea.
3 for $3.00

NEW ADDRESS:
2812 BAYONNE DR.
PALM BEACH GARDENS, FL 33410

Please send me:

Name _____

Address _____

State _____ Zip_____

	Price	Shipping	Total
☐ Sewing For Profits	$10.00	$1.00	
☐ Teenage Moneymaking Guide ...	$10.00	$1.00	
☐ How To Sell Your Homemade Creation	$11.95	$1.50	
☐ How To Make School Fun	$10.00	$1.50	
Coffee Cups ☐ ____ ____ (Amount) (Type)	2/$5.00	$1.50	
Bumper Stickers ☐ ____ ____ (Amount) (Type)	3/$3.00	.50	

☐ Payment Enclosed Total _____
☐ Master/Visa

☐☐☐☐☐☐☐☐☐☐☐☐☐☐☐☐

Exp. Date _____

☐ Signature _____

HOW TO MAKE SCHOOL FUN

12 Oz.
Coffee
Mug

Reg.
$2.95

Special
2/$5.00

Bumper Stickers
$1.25 ea.
2 for $3.00